Teenage Reading

Edited by
Peter Kennerley

Ward Lock Educational

ISBN 0 7062 3889 3

First published 1979

Set in 11 on 13 point Monotype Garamond
Printed by Hollen Street Press Ltd, Slough, Berkshire
for Ward Lock Educational
116 Baker Street, London W1M 2BB
A member of the Pentos Group
Made in Great Britain

Contents

Part Four   Guidelines

Foreword

What writers have to say lies in their books, not in articles about writing, or books for this and that category, or books that tell you what other people think, or what you should think.

If it is your aim to bring children and books together and create the habit of reading in the young so that they like reading, then it is essential that you are such a reader yourself, with the habit of reading, and that you know the world of books that you yourself find absorbing, particularly fiction, so that you have developed a sense of discernment. Secondly, it is just as important that you have read and understood by those same criteria the books made available to the readers you are hoping to encourage. Thirdly, you should know those young as individuals, and only then can you perhaps match the book to the individual.

There are no simple answers, no oughts and musts and shoulds and don'ts, but the first proviso is truly essential; without it, all books such as this one are more than useless.

Joan Tate

Introduction

Monday to Friday I am an English teacher in a college of education; at weekends and in the holidays, and sometimes in the early hours of the morning, I am the editor of a magazine about children's books. In one sense I live in two distinct worlds: one of teaching and one of publishing. These two worlds ought to show considerable overlap, but all too frequently they do not. If he is doing his job properly, the teacher ought to be deeply knowledgeable about books, the publisher, and the children's book world in general, and he ought to be deeply involved with children. At one glance, I see an exciting, stimulating, sensitive range of books; on the other, all too frequently, I see children in secondary schools who are taking no pleasure and satisfaction from books.

This book grew out of my sense of frustration. I felt certain that many people from different fields were necessary to each other if we were to begin to solve the problem of young teenagers capable of reading, but unwilling to read. Co-operation between the world of books and the world of education lies at the centre of this project.

In **Part One, Overview**, three different people consider some of the basic issues concerned with teenage reading – the problems, the content, the characteristics. Geoffrey Summerfield, until July 1979, was teaching at the University of York, David Homer, an Australian working for a year at York has replied to Geoffrey Summerfield's case. Aidan Chambers occupies a unique position in the realm of children's books in that for ten years he was a teacher before becoming a writer and founder of the Topliner series of teenage paperbacks.

Part Two, The Books, begins with ideas from Rosemary Sandberg, a discerning children's editor, and continues with statements from four important writers: Robert Westall, Paul Zindel, Jill Paton Walsh and Robert Cormier. Robert Leeson, writer and critic, has considered the role of the critic – children and teenagers tend not to read reviews, so what is the function of the reviewer?

Television and film are of immense significance in drawing young viewers into books, and Peter Plummer, a highly talented director with Granada, has written about television adaptation of novels.

Part Three, the Readers, moves into the schools to present a range of experience and ideas from educationalists and librarians. Trevor Dickinson is an HMI whose concern for children's books is widely known. David Burns is an English Adviser in Gloucestershire. John L. Foster is an editor, a writer, and a headmaster. Keith Stevens is Education Librarian in Newcastle, and Cecilia Gordon has recently retired after many years as a school librarian.

In **Part Four, Guidelines**, Chris Kloet, Young People's Librarian for Tameside, contributes an A–Z of Fiction for Teenagers. Because of the large number of titles, authors and themes listed, this section is likely to be of considerable practical help to the teacher who is selecting books for class or library use.

Part One
Overview

1 'Oh the impossibility of books-for-adolescents'
Geoffrey Summerfield

> The imperfect is our paradise.
> Note that, in this bitterness, delight,
> Since the imperfect is so hot in us,
> Lies in flawed words . . .
> *Wallace Stevens*

Of all the seven ages of man, however you measure them, adolescence is the most emphatically imperfect: as one of my students said the other day, 'I felt such a failure!' Or, as Scott Fitzgerald put it in a letter to his erring adolescent daughter: 'The adolescent knows nothing, does nothing, that the adult cannot know and do better'.

Of books that have recently given me great pleasure, the most memorable and deeply resonant are: Ted Hughes' *Gaudete*; Raymond Briggs' *Fungus the Bogeyman*; Hesketh Pearson's *The Smith of Smiths*; Randall Jarell's *Third Book of Criticism*; Darwin's *Journal of a Voyage Round the World*; Jacques Lipchitz's *My Life in Sculpture*; Lillian Hellman's *Scoundrel Time*; *The Bear Who Wanted To Stay a Bear*, and *The Shrinking of Treehorn*. These oddly various books strike me on this occasion as having one negative characteristic in common – they are *not* books that I would be inclined to recommend to, or share with, adolescent readers. Each of these texts is either too simple or too complex, too childish or too adult: the kinds of books that would be dismissed by most adolescents with a shrug of indifference, scorn, or incomprehension.

If adolescence is primarily a socio-biological phenomenon, it is also a cultural construct, and the processes whereby society 'creates' adolescence have been intensified in the last twenty years to a degree that constitutes almost a difference of kind. One has to think only of Jules Henry's *Culture Against Man* to be reminded of how insistently the confused sensibilities of adolescence are strafed and saturated by the commercial armies of the West. What were your adolescent hopes, fears, anxieties, obsessions, and delights, dear reader? How often were they reinforced, picked at, opened up, titillated, by the magazines that you carried off to your bedroom to read in private? Those of us who slouched and drooped through adolescence twenty or more years ago will probably need to multiply our case tenfold, even a hundredfold, to gain some measure of the degree to which teen-magazines try to narrow the focus of their readers to a dozen or so obsessively recurrent questions – How 'pretty' is my nose? How sparkling are my eyes? How closely does my body approximate to the currently fashionable norms – those norms which for older narcissists are represented, in a poshly pernicious way, by the glittering pages of *Vogue*? Why don't I have a boyfriend? If I do , how far should we 'go'? Does my body smell? And so on.

How accurately and naggingly do these teen-mags home in on the preoccupations of modern adolescence! And how they single out girls as their especial market. As a woman student observed to me, of her sense even at fourteen of being 'picked on' for exploitation, 'I *knew* it wasn't fair'. Again, how unpredictable are the mercurial moods and vagaries of adolescents; how difficult it is for adults to sustain a consistent, genial, equable relationship with them. And, of course, few adults can write extensively of the frets, the fevers, the ecstacies, the moods of these years without falsification, or boredom, or tendentiousness. When a writer really does put a finger on the pulse, as in *Le Grand Meaulnes*, one is struck by a sense almost of miraculous tact, patience, and scrupulous fidelity. So, for every hundred successful chapters on childhood, in *bildungsroman* literature, we are lucky to find just one or two on adolescence: even the rhetoric of the adolescent is *sui generis*, impossible to fabricate and fatally easy to caricature.

When forced into a corner and constrained to tell the truth, I have to admit that after five or six years of untroubled absorption in the seemingly inexhaustible pages of Arthur Mee's *Children's Encyclopedia*, Percy F. Westerman, Rafael Sabatini, and the *1001 Nights*, I precipitately lunged at the age of thirteen into the subtly oblique complexities of *Madame Bovary*. Even the name had a wickedly suggestive aura, mysteriously redolent of ovaries. After fifty pages I admitted defeat, and so turned away from books almost entirely for the space of about three years – except, that is, for the *longeurs* of class-readers in school. The mature Matthew Arnold proposed that literature is a criticism of life; but in adolescence we may discover, albeit temporarily, that life is, contrariwise, a criticism of literature. Amazingly, many erstwhile child-bookworms find real life to be too vivid, urgent, multicoloured, magnetic, insistent, compelling, too nervously alive to allow much time for the silent and solitary pleasures of the printed word – especially those sanctioned by well-meaning adults – to stand a chance. And in the case of those adolescents who continue to turn to literature for succour, pleasure, anticipations of adulthood, the kinds of books they choose would make dedicated readers of *The Use of English* throw up their hands in comminatory horror.

My students, in conversation, confirm my notion that my experience was not, in the event, all that eccentric: 'I stopped reading altogether for a year or so'. 'I stopped reading, except for "junk" such as *Skinhead*, which we used to pass around, with the "dirty bits" marked.' 'I didn't enjoy school-literature, but I went in for "comfortable" reading, and read all of Enid Blyton all over again.' 'I was in a state of continual fermentation, and read very little.' These are the reports of university students of English, all of whom achieved very good results in English A level. Most of them browsed, often privately, even furtively, in *True Romances* and teen-magazines, and turned to books primarily for a romantic representation of courtship and love: their privately favoured authors at fifteen were: Juliet Benzoni, Catherine Cookson, Georgette Heyer, Mazo de la Roche, Jean Plaidy, Anya Seton, and Lucilla Andrews, the 'Sue Barton' and 'Cherry Ames' novelettes, and the Mills and Boon titles: romantic fiction for unsophisticated adult women.

Those who continued to read for pleasure through their adolescence moved indiscriminately between Orwell, Graham Greene, Dickens, D. H. Lawrence, Hardy, the Brontës, the teen-magazines, especially *Jackie*, and women's magazines, especially for their problem-pages. 'But how could you spend time and money on *Jackie*?' I asked one. 'Simply because I could genuinely, truly, relate to it.'

Whatever your criteria for a definition of adolescence – biological, biochemical, developmental, social, cultural, or whatever – it will have to recognize the irreversible magnitude of the deep and perplexing transformations that occur there: and admit also the unprecedented intensities of its loving, hating, longing, grieving, self-pitying confusions, its moods and its energies: its crisis-riddledness. All these are, of course, common knowledge, often unexpressed. And it seems that we 'work' so hard to break through to 'maturity', to a state of moving on a more or less even keel that we succeed in suppressing much of this inherently transient knowledge – a knowledge that is so much more vivid than the cognitive tracts of the school curriculum: the knowledge of deep uncertainty, of intense self-love and self-loathing – all the whirligig of feelings that are at times almost too much, and spill over into the scribbling of 'poetry' – 'the high-wrought enthusiasm of fancy and feeling', as Hazlitt called it – and the rambling narcissism of the diary. If you say that I exaggerate, I reply that you forget. As Wallace Steven wrote, of other matters, in *Notes Toward a Supreme Fiction*: 'We are shaken by them ... We reason about them with a later reason'. And our 'later reason', for a variety of reasons, often fails to register the sheer promiscuity of the 'literature' of adolescence – an extraordinary mixture of good, bad, and indifferent, accepted quite indiscriminately after the fashion of Keats's chameleon-poet. It is only later, in our more judicious years, that we turn moral philosopher and delude ourselves into believing that we really did love only the best that has been thought and said and the moral ironies of this amnesia have never received the attention they deserve. As Jerome Singer, of Yale, observed of adolescent fantasy: there seems to be almost a conspiracy of silence about it.

It follows, therefore, that after the constant, recurring, communal archetypes and paradigms of childhood's myths and fictions, the more or less clearly pre-ordained salient features of the stories of the blissfully androgynous years, wherein, as Vladimir Propp has so well argued, character is little more than narrative-function; it follows that with the sudden individuation, privatization, and intensification of puberty, there can be no *satisfactory* 'literature for adolescents' since, *a priori*, there can be no such thing as 'literature for adolescents'. If, then, we take a look at popular books for adolescent readers (popular, that is, with booksellers, parents, and teachers), what do we find?

On the one hand, an ersatz, limiting, banal, provincial brand of 'social realism', a kind of literature of repressive tolerance – 'We will allow you this much sex, or violence, or passion, or anarchy, or whatever; so much, and no more'; on the other, the factitious pseudo-fantasies of Alan Garner and Richard Adams. I don't know which is worse: Garner with his gaucheness, narrational incompetence, unrealized settings, tricks of transition, implausibilities, and creaking dialogue; or Adams, with his boring epics, his willed tendentiousness, his linguistic uncertainties, and his literary heritage. If, moreover, we *teach* literature and cannot contemplate spending our years in offering such meretriciousness, then we 'guide' pupils through texts which demand interminable explanation and significance-underlining, dragging them into the darker, deeper mysteries of D. H. Lawrence's bloodstream, for the worst of reasons – that such explicatory talk satisfies our own need for moral significance and missionary zeal. So we fall headlong into the trap so well described by James Agee in *Let Us Now Praise Famous Men*: 'It would be hard to make clear enough the deadliness of vacuum and apathy which is closed over the very nature of teaching, over teachers and pupils alike: or in what different worlds words and processes leave a teacher, and reach a child ... [the pupils'] intelligence becomes hopelessly bewildered, drawn off its centres, bored, or atrophied'.

All I wish to offer is the distinctly modest and muted wisdom offered to Little Bo Peep:

> Leave them alone,
> And they'll come home,
> Wagging their tales behind them.

One day, lo and behold, a sixteen, or seventeen-year old (one in ten? twenty?) gropes her way into *Ulysses*, or *The Golden Notebook*, *Kinflicks* or *Radcliffe*, and rediscovers the peculiar distinctive powers of the fictive imagination. Unpredictably, happily, fiction has come back into its own. And once again, after the year or two of wandering through the strange inner landscapes of introspection, of privacy, of alienation, the young burgeoning reader returns to rejoin the community of those who, without affectation, know for themselves the truth of Henry James's insistence that to appreciate a work of art is to make it your own.

Meanwhile, the examination system and its functionaries will doubtless continue to have the last word and put many potential readers off literature for life. And the virtually inexhaustible treasures of autobiography, the one field within which adolescents could

7

continue to relate with the written word – these treasures will continue to be mostly consigned to outer darkness since they constitute merely a rather low-status sub-department of literature, even when they are let in. But that is another question.

2 The possibilities of literature for adolescents
David Homer

> The miracle is not that we are all deformed by the dominant
> culture of our society but how much grows in the teeth of it . . .
>
> *Harold Rosen*

On my desk at the moment are a dozen or so novels which, in the
best paperback traditions, have interesting covers and arresting
titles. There is Alice Childress' *A Hero Ain't Nothin' but a Sandwich*;
Nat Hentoff's *I'm Really Dragged But Nothing Gets Me Down*; Judy
Blume's *Starring Sally J Freedman as Herself*; Paul Zindel's *I Never
Loved Your Mind*; Richard Peck's *Are You in the House Alone?* There
is a fine novel by an adolescent writer, S. E. Hinton, called *The
Outsiders* which is set in the culture of an urban neighbourhood gang.
These books have a number of things in common. All, I would
argue, contain interesting, sympathetic and well written stories which
are used to explore the themes of adolescent existence: conflict
with parents, peer group pressures, the demands of school, drugs,
abortion, unlikely sources of happiness, seemingly opposed value
systems, and so on.

They are not gimmicky. Any one provides ample material for the
discussion of several of the themes mentioned, in school or elsewhere.
They exhibit and exploit a wide range of narrative modes and techniques, especially those which deploy an 'I' narrator, or which shift
the narrative point of view to provide a number of different per-
spectives on events. They don't preach or 'talk down'. They do not
embody ideologies contrary to the proof of the events described.
They demonstrate adolescents' existential experience very clearly
and little else. They are popular with adolescent readers. Just these
dozen or so books make nonsense of any claim that there can be no
satisfactory literature for adolescents. They have, by the way, one
more common characteristic. All of them are American.

The claims I have made for this American fiction for adolescents,

9

however, can only partly answer Geoffrey Summerfield's statement. It is a hard position with which to engage, slipping and dodging as it does in and out of literature and non-literature, novel and anecdote, general and particular experience. Perhaps the best thing to do is admit that there's a lot of truth in what he says but that much of it needs serious qualification.

Of course adolescents can be 'impossible' and can themselves find life impossible, as any parent or teacher knows. Adolescents' search for a satisfactory place in the world *may* result in life becoming a criticism of literature, but this would be far from true for all adolescents. All of us know some adolescents who do not give up the reading habit, albeit their tastes may change and vaccilate as do their tastes in friends, sports, clothes and hero-figures. But even if we were to admit that adult writers find it difficult, or even impossible to adequately capture adolescent experiences in literature (which I do not believe to be the case) we are surely ignoring a lot of what literature potentially can be both in itself, and in its provision of satisfaction to readers. It's not what literature is about that counts, it's what we make of it: with literature, serious is as serious does.

We have had the argument that you've got to be living it to write satisfactorily about it in connection with ethnic and feminist literature. By its terms we would have to exclude most Children's Literature as well as that for adolescents. Authors write what they know, only that. Readers can only say from their point of view: 'He got it wrong (or right)'. I don't happen to believe that D. H. Lawrence got things particularly right, but I cannot deny the nature of his knowing, nor the experience of those readers who think that he did. I don't see that the situation is any different for those who write for adolescents or their readers.

There can be, and is, a satisfactory literature for adolescents and in fact Geoffrey Summerfield tells us what some of it is. It is *Jackie*, it is Catherine Cookson, it is Georgette Heyer (we are told, but I doubt it), it is *True Romance* magazines and a host of things which would make the 'readers of *The Use of English* throw up their hands in comminatory horror'. From personal experience I would say it also includes material about war, Science Fiction and technical literature, particularly about cars and motor bikes. And there is a fair sprinkling of soft-core pornography both in the form of novels and magazines. Much of it may be 'romantic fiction for unsophisticated adults' but if it is read by adolescents then it is *for* them as well, something in which they can find at least momentary satisfaction. Just because one's real life concerns are immediately sexuality, social roles, self-image, it doesn't mean a satisfactory literature for you is necessarily about these things. The provision of fictional alternatives to current experience is a major role of literature in society (however we define either), for child, adult and adolescent. And what is a motor-bike magazine but a fictional alternative?

But Summerfield is guilty of more than overgeneralization. Having said that no adult writer can satisfactorily treat adolescent experience, (and thus strongly suggested that what he means is that there can be no *significant* literature for adolescents), he has an each-way bet and says that even if they could, no adolescent would want to read it. He sees adolescent experience as so multivarious and so tied to the minute that literature has nothing to say in relation to it. I have already claimed that many adolescents *do* read, often widely, often, maybe, indiscriminately and eclectically. But if we take him up on his own grounds, on the grounds of literature which is 'seriously' for and about adolescents, then there is the same problem of over-generalization, for he sees the offering as hovering between the two ends of a highly improbable spectrum.

I would hate to think that there was no more to it than an 'unsatisfactory form of social realism' and 'the factitious pseudo-fantasies of Richard Adams and Alan Garner' (and I don't think this is true of *The Owl Service* or *Red Shift*). He gives no examples of unsatisfactory novels of social realism and hence no reasons why they are 'ersatz, limiting, banal (and) provincial'. Now I would want to say that much of Paul Zindel's work, or a book like Paula Fox's *Blowfish Live in the Sea* present far from ersatz views of adolescent social reality, because many adolescent readers have told me so. It's the same with *Catcher in the Rye*. 'Satisfactory' or not, we could hardly deny that it is a fully serious attempt to capture adolescent experience. That it succeeds as a 'read' for adolescents is measured by the number of them who can 'genuinely, truly relate to it'. Geoffrey Summerfield forgets, I think, not his experience as an adolescent reader but his experience as a teacher. Surely good teaching is recognizing what books 'help' at the time, and then helping students to see why.

While I doubt that many teachers (or adults generally) when pressed would want to maintain that they have always loved only the greatest and best in literature, there *is* a tendency among them, born out of the degree system and sired by English departments to feel guilty if their charges are not studying 'quality' literature. School reading lists, speech day prizes and countless dust-gathering birthday presents bear witness to this phobia. Some insane literary atrocities are worked upon the minds of adolescents in school, reaching a peak, I think, in the fourth and fifth years of secondary education, especially among those seriously pursuing the examinations path. At the peak of adolescent turmoil, when experience is generating its most extreme criticisms of literature and everything else in life, the school's literary fare is at its furthest from the individual's dietary needs.

One thing the school could do more fully during these years, is to recognize *what* adolescents are reading and base its programmes on that. In this sense, non-examination classes sometimes get a better deal than their more 'fortunate' peers, for their teachers often *do* work from their current reading and concerns, and the work is a continuation of that done in the junior forms. Australian students, who do not by and large have to face a public examination until the end of their sixth year, also are served slightly better. Of course it's very often not the books themselves that are the problem, but the teaching associated with them. Despite the many advances made in literature teaching in the past fifteen years, there remains a tendency among many teachers to erect boring and inhibiting barriers between student readers and their reading experience.

So when I say that there is a literature for adolescents, I am saying that much of it is, by some definition, non-literature (i.e. comics, magazines) and some of it may be – by literary or academic 'standards' – trivial. That its importance to adolescents is ignored and denigrated is a shame. But what of the 'other' kind of literature, which Geoffrey Summerfield says can not be written? Serious literature for and about adolescence is similarly ignored by examination syllabuses.

I cannot accept his caricaturization of fiction for adolescents, but I do think that it points to a problem in the writing for this audience, which has been more squarely faced in the United States than it has in Britain and Australia. Summerfield implies that the 'failure' is a failure not of relevance, but one of 'capture' – it is not possible for an author to adequately realize adolescent experience in literary form. He doesn't develop the idea far but I think had he done so he could have shown that the problem of relevance in fiction for adolescents is not encountered at the level of subject matter, but within narrative mode and structure, the standpoint taken in the transformation of raw to literary experience.

Let us begin by examining two passages, first from William Mayne's *A Game of Dark*, and then Alice Childress' *A Hero Ain't Nothin' But a Sandwich*. In the first, Donald (Jackson) visits his dying, crippled father in hospital:

The nurse smiled at him and said 'Is it your grandpa?' and went away.

Donald looked at the man on the bed, who turned his head and looked back at him for a moment, and then turned wearily away. It was a stranger, Donald thought, some one who did not belong to him at all, some one unknown and recently appeared, with whom he had no part. But still, in the run of time, this was the man who had raced about in a wheel chair and made racing car noises to amuse a small boy. Perhaps the small boy was no longer there either, and there were two unacquainted people in this communal bedroom with its separate territories and divisions horizontally into the space under the high beds and the space above, and all the people shared the narrow layer between bed height and a man's standing height.

But this was the racing car man, and this was the small boy, and they did belong to each other, though not across the present, only through each other's past.

Mrs Jackson came back and told Donald to say goodbye for now and wait in the entrance hall of that wing of the hospital. Then she sat down again. The words of goodbye came out of Donald's mouth and were lost in the ward, and not noticed. He went out of the room, down the stairs, and waited in a lower hall.

In half an hour Mrs Jackson came out again. 'He refused his injection,' she said. 'But he took it in the end, and he was much better for it. He has a great deal of pain. He said he was sorry for not saying much to you, and now he's asleep.'

Donald said nothing. A flutter of guilt and gladness and association moved in his throat and squeezed behind his eyes so that

13

they moistened. He swallowed a spasm of muscle that might have
been a sob, and walked mistily out of the building beside Mrs
Jackson.

The novel examines a number of typically adolescent problems
surrounding the guilt which accompanies growing independence and
self-awareness, the rationalizations associated with these (such as the
possibilities of being adopted or illegitimate) and the difficulty of
reconciling a religion of love with the reality of suffering. Mayne
explores the problems by examining them in juxtaposition with
Donald's fantasy world in which he wrestles with the demands of
honour, tradition and chivalry as the squire of a knight assigned to
kill a monstrous worm, while at the same time experiencing the
pressures of social responsibility (the worm is killing people) and
sexual loyalty. Mayne merges Donald's worlds brilliantly, and they
acquire equally 'real' status, largely through manipulation of symbols.
It is a technique with which British writers seem particularly adept;
one has only to think of novels like *Red Shift* and *Tom's Midnight
Garden*.

In the section from Alice Childress' novel, we hear Jimmy Lee
Powell consider his life, and that of his friend Benjie, a thirteen-year-
old heroin addict. Jimmy Lee's is one of a dozen voices heard in the
novel, all as interior or dramatic monologues.

A social worker is somebody who makes they bread and fame
offa other people's troubles. Lotta people plannin to make it as a
social worker, cause the field is so wide-ass open, and trouble,
accordin to Benjie's grandma, is somethin that's sure gonna last
always. Hell, I could be a social worker myself! When a junkie gets
real messed up, the thorities send them into talk groups to get
talked to. What you think they talkin bout? Just tellin how they
papa and mama don't understand, and they also be saying 'ghetto'
and things like that. Benjie gonna be brainwash with that crap.
Right now, he try to tell me how his daddy run off and how that
make him a child from a broken home. Shit! Sometime I wish my
home was broke. Benjie don't know how to dig good luck! He's
got a stepfather who's bringin in a color TV and hi-fi record
player and all kinda good things people need. True, Mr Butler
Craig gives him talkins to bout don't do this and don't do that,

damn, the man titled to say somethin. But Benjie steady complainin bout havin a step and a broken home.

Both of these passages deal urgently with adolescent problems, but do so very differently. This is not the place to conjecture about the different directions taken by writers of fiction for adolescents in Britain and Australia on the one hand, and America on the other, but it may be useful to characterize their different approaches to narrative relevance. As far as I can see, both groups of writers are willing to face adolescent dilemmas pretty squarely. Colin Theile's *The Fire in the Stone* (set in the tough Andamoeka opal fields of South Australia), Ivan Southall's *Josh*, Alan Garner's *The Owl Service*, William Mayne's *Ravensgill* are no less clear about adolescents' experience than Paul Zindel's *My Darling, My Hamburger* or Paula Fox's *Blowfish Live in the Sea*. But the narrative treatment is very different. If I can indulge in a generalization I would say that British and Australian writers prefer to represent adolescent concerns at a symbolic level, and thus need anonymous, omniscient, manipulative narrators and local (often rural) settings with just such rich symbolic (through myth, legend, and folk tale) potential. American writers for adolescents seem to prefer identified narrators and a literal journalistic mode of description. They use more direct speech and present a more concrete, less evaluative narrative, usually in an urban setting.

Obviously both groups of writers have their following among adolescents and neither shows any sign of going out of business. It is not a question of relative literary merits (if in fact these could be defined), but I suspect that the *greatest* enthusiasms for writers like Mayne, Garner and Southall are shown by adults because what they write is adult literature. I say this with the greatest respect to their mailbags which must contain many letters from appreciative adolescents. One pleasure of mature, adult reading is provided by the way a narrative is constructed and presented so that the events embody their own evaluation. Now no text can be ideologically neutral, but I would say that in America there exists a substantial body of literature for adolescents in which evaluation is subordinated to narrative.

The American linguist William Labov has shown quite clearly that adolescent oral narrative is relatively (to adult) non-evaluative of the events described. As with other forms of language use, narrative fulfils different kinds of needs and it may well be that American writers for adolescents show a more satisfactory sense of the narrative needs of their readers than their British counterparts. The geographical generalization may be difficult to maintain, but the point about narrative is not.

In childhood, narrative serves a representational function; it is an ordering process by which the individual is able to get clear what has happened (and indeed what happens generally). I think that what we might say of the unpredictable reading habits of adolescents is that they are a result of an increasing dissatisfaction with the largely ordering function and the beginning of a search for a further functional dimension, the use of narrative to evaluate experience. Hence the importance to them of a variety of literature in which evaluation is essentially non-problematic (as in Catherine Cookson *et al*), or, in which there is at least a fairly obvious freedom to impose one's own. In other words, Geoffrey Summerfield might be right to claim a kind of impossibility about attempts to write for adolescents, but the situation which he describes may not be as random as he claims. Indeed, if literature (authors) and the school (teachers) are going to continue to try to do anything to help individuals make any sense of their lives during adolescence, then the problems of writing for them will need continued attention.

If we accept that education should help adolescents build some kind of understanding of their individuality in relation to the social reality of their existence, then we need literature. We simply can't do without it. If we accept, with M. A. K. Halliday, that such understanding is largely built functionally, through language, then literature (of all kinds) emerges as a major resource. If we further accept that at least in an ideal situation there is an agreement between teacher and student that this is what we are on about, then consideration of the function of reading can be seen as a wholly valid way of achieving this aim. Summerfield sketches an unhappily accurate context for the treatment of literature in school but it does not have to be this way at all. I know few young adolescents who couldn't make more sense of the ending of Ivan Southall's *Josh* than any of their social studies texts!

Josh provides a good example of what I mean. Josh emerges from the horror of the unfamiliar world of Ryan Creek, with its inexplicable kids, and the unreasonable Plowman code of behaviour. Aunt Clara tells him that everything is all right now, can't he see this? Josh can't. He knows that she still expects things of him which he cannot accept and he rejects her demands, knowing that in her eyes and those of the townspeople his status will be diminished. But a reader can see that he is in fact prepared to trade this respect for the new strength he has gained whilst amongst them. In a teaching relationship where it is legitimate to consider what can be salvaged from 'failure', and how success is always relative, a stage in a wider process, *Josh* may be an important text. At least it gives some teachers, and some adolescent students a chance.

My reply to Geoffrey Summerfield is that authors and teachers and adolescents will continue to try to achieve the impossible. It is also to say that it is not as impossible as he says. Literature may be a criticism of life, but reading, viewing and listening for adolescents is *part of life* to be coped with along with life's other aspects. In fact, in societies hooked on schooling as the major sanctioned educative process, and which demand that schools help their students make some sense of their social existence, where else can the dialogue begin *but* with literature? Suitable literature does exist, and of course not all of this is written exclusively *for* adolescents. It seems to me that the problem is not so much the 'impossibility of literature for adolescents' but the impossibilities created by home, school and societal sanctions in terms of what you are able to say (or think, or admit) about whatever it is that you *do* read.

3 Alive and flourishing: a personal view of teenage literature

Aidan Chambers

I have never experienced any difficulty with the idea of a literature for adolescents. On the contrary: all my working life, first as a teacher, then as an editor and author, such a literature has not only seemed necessary but possible, not only possible but *there*. It already exists: is written, published, read, and has been for a great many years. The rather curious, not to say eccentric, opposition to 'teenage books' has always, it seems to me, ducked this fact that the literature has a history. Indeed, the argument against teenage books is really only intelligent as an argument against children's and young people's books as a whole.

Let's settle the historical point first. As long ago as 1802 Sarah Trimmer, that vigorous educationalist whose *Guardian of Education* was the first journal seriously to review children's books in any systematic fashion, wrote in an article entitled 'Observations on the Changes Which Have Taken Place in Books for Children and Young Persons' that, when discussing books published for the young, we should:

> endeavour to separate them into two distinct classes, *viz*. Books *for children*, and Books *for Young Persons*; but where to draw the line may be the question: formerly, all were reckoned *children*, till they had at least attained their *fourteenth year*. Now, if we may judge from the titles of many little volumes, compared with their contents, we have *Young Persons* of *five* or *six years old*. However, in our arrangement [. . .] we shall, without regard to *title pages*, take the liberty of adopting the idea of our forefathers, by supposing all young gentlemen and ladies to be *children*, till they are *fourteen* and *young persons* till they are at least *twenty-one*; and shall class the books we examine as they shall appear to us to be suitable to these different stages of human life.

Nothing much changes: Sarah's forefathers well understood about adolescence; Sarah saw the need to separate the books into those for children and those for teenagers; and yet still we ring the changes on the argument about whether there can be or is a literature for young people! The truth is that by the time Jane Austen was composing *Northanger Abbey* (her own make-use of her adolescent pop reading) teenage books were well under way. Soon some still-remembered names and still-read examples of the form were coming out: Marryat's *Masterman Ready* in 1841; Charlotte Younge's *The Heir of Redclyffe* in 1853; Hughes's influential *Tom Brown's Schooldays* in 1857; Kingsley's *Hereward the Wake* in 1866; Ballantyne's sequence of youthful adventures – a high point in the Victorian version of teenage travails – then Henty, of course, and on to the first of the early moderns: Talbot Baines Reed, with Henry Rider Haggard only a step behind, and Stevenson, the master, the peak of achievement, after which you either follow in the master's footsteps, as some still do, or look for refreshment, new avenues, different approaches.

In only a hundred years an honourable enough tradition was established for a literature which all through that time was only uneasily accepted, despite the amount of it written and read, of which the names I've mentioned are but a reminder. As always in every art, most of the work produced has sunk without trace, leaving the peaks to be admired.

I had not heard of Mrs Trimmer or that long historical pedigree when I attained Young Personhood. But I loved Reed, enjoyed Ballantyne, admired especially Twain's *Huckleberry Finn* and read great quantities of stuff I cannot now recall as individual books but only as a kind of emotional sludge: stories about life at sea (I had a patch of wanting to follow in my grandfather's mercantile footsteps), life in Africa (*Prester John* and *King Solomon's Mines* started that) and then found the greatest teenage book of them all, *Sons and Lovers*, when life changed a bit, and my reading with it. Colette with her older women making men of boys was unaccountably attractive for a while. I did not think of any of these as teenage books, of course. But I liked them because they talked about me, or so I thought. And I took note of the extra pleasure I got from the deeper attention I gave to books which connected directly with my current state of being.

Before we get too scornful of that, let's just examine our own latter-day reading. *Daniel Martin*, I have to confess, completely absorbed me for a whole week recently. By some critical standards it might be thought too long, a little self-indulgently rangey. I'll bet its editor wanted it cut. But, frankly, I couldn't care less; it could have gone on for another two hundred pages as far as I'm concerned. For why? Because it is about being middle-aged and working in the arts in England in the present time. There is a great deal, too, about the differences between England and America, about young people now, and that whole fascinating business of being born into the rural working class and educated into the declassed professional urban ways. This year I'm forty-four, am married to an American and have a fair bit to do with the USA; I was born into the semi-rural working class and was educated into the professions; I'm surrounded in everything I do by young people just into their twenties who exercise a large measure of say in what happens to my work. Is there any wonder that Daniel Martin seemed like a pal? If that's all right for me-and-literature, then it is all right for teenagers and what they want to read too.

Let me pause to clarify one point which always bedevils discussion of children's and teenage books. I do *not* believe teenage literature is *only* for children or teenagers; I do *not* believe that young people should *only* read what is published for them, and nothing else. Far from it. The sooner children and teenagers reach into the mainstream of our literature the better. But I do believe that most people will reach into it more vigorously, more willingly, and with deeper understanding of the pleasures it offers if they have encountered on the way a literature which is for them, in at least the way I've just described, and which is written and published with as much dedication and skill as is the best of the mainstream work.

I do not believe either, incidentally, that children and teenagers are different kinds of beings from adults. They are all people. The difference lies in the fact that children live at least part of their lives seeing things from a different point of view from teenagers and adults; they place the emphasis of concern and interest on different aspects of life, and so too do teenagers from children and adults. For that reason, *Catcher in the Rye*, although first published for adults, has become a standard work of teenage literature. And quite rightly; it is in teenage that it carries most impact. Similarly, *The Mouse and*

His Child, though published for children is gradually settling down as a book most favoured in the teen years. It all has to do with an alchemy based on the elements of tone, content, point of view, thematic concerns, language and textual reference points.

Typically, the argument jams up at this point for lack of a critical apparatus commonly known to all of us interested in the question under discussion. And we lack it because endless disparagement of the form by people who, for whatever reasons, dismiss it as beyond serious interest – a bastard and unwanted hybrid – has frightened off those who are equipped with the training, skills and knowledge to build the critical approaches that might help. They wouldn't want to be thought academically retarded for handling such apparently unrespectable material. Thus work as diverse and honourable as Alan Garner's *The Owl Service*, William Corlett's trilogy beginning with *The Gate of Eden*, and Virginia Hamilton's novels (to name no more) are airily and ignorantly dismissed without a moment's hesitant glance because they appear as books for young people.

I left myself a few paragraphs back at the classroom door. I'll pick myself up there again, but this time going in as a teacher. I have recorded some of the results of the first few years of my teaching career in *The Reluctant Reader* and will not bore you with them again. Teenage books as a bridge between children's and adult literature was the initial impelling idea behind Topliners and the beginning of my accidentally acquired career as an editor. As one Topliner reader wrote, explaining why he liked them, 'It is a big step up from Blyton to Doetovsky'. If you haven't made it by the time you are twelve you need help. That being so for the majority of people, I reasoned, why should the 'bridge books' be any less well written and produced than the mass of books in the general trade lists? Why should they be, if anything at all, self-consciously and apologetically 'educational' products, produced by people whose aims were pedagogic rather than literary, and by firms more expert in manufacturing textbooks to satisfy the peculiarities of a teacher in a classroom than in the making of books intended for the pleasure of a reader-at-home? For better or worse the result was Topliners.

Very quickly, however, I came to see that teenage literature was not simply about bridging, a kind of literary remedial course. It could do, and should do, what any literature that is whole does: grow to satisfy writers and readers in increasingly multifarious ways, responding to its own history, to other arts, and to the needs of its own time. Topliner readers led me to that recognition: to the possibilities for teenage literature. From the start they wrote letters about the books; they still arrive at the rate of a couple of dozen a week – with the occasional daunting, not to say appalling, class-load. 'Dear Editor, our teacher said we had to write and tell you what we thought of . . .' Spontanaeity of response is one thing, forced marches to the post box are another.

Certain features are common to most of the willingly written letters. Let me list them. The majority like best stories which are about: people roughly their own age; contemporary times; the obvious, but none the less potent, themes: parental relationships, challenging authority, establishing one's own personality and future, relationships with peers and (when allowed in a literature still puritanically controlled by the intermediary adults) sex.

So far, so predictable; but there is a pressure point less explicitly articulated and which, writing replies to the weekly mail, one begins to feel with increasing seriousness. There is a between-the-lines statement: 'I know what I like but want to be taken further'. As a question, it is often put this way: 'Could you tell me what other books of this kind I would enjoy?' The idea that people want more of the same all the time is not actually true, I think. Not in this context at least. What they are asking for, I've learned, is not just a repetition of the pleasure but *a deepening and an expansion of it*.

A personal parallel to help make the point: I mentioned earlier my reading of *Daniel Martin*. Shortly after reading that novel I enjoyed also John Wain's *The Pardoner's Tale*, most of Iris Murdoch's *The Sea, the Sea*, and found myself then unexpectedly wanting to reread Graham Greene's *The End of the Affair*. The overlapping connections between those books are pretty plain and – my point – I know I enjoyed each of them all the more because of the contrasting presence of the others. I would have got less from each if I had not read the others. That is a commonplace phenomenon and in my view it is an essential event in truly literary reading. All the more important, then, that young people experience it and grow literarily thereby. But to make possible an enhancing multiplicity of narratives, the books must be written, published, and be widely available: there must be a teenage literature, not just a few books that happen by chance to be especially liked by teenagers.

The need for such books I knew from my own teenage years and from my time as a teacher. The publishing possibility I learned from my work as an editor. But everything depends in the end on writers who want to write such books.

At the time of touting the idea of Topliners fourteen years ago, I was told by all sorts of people – publishers, librarians, booksellers – that there was not only no market for teenage books but that no writers worth their muse would want to write them. It is still said. Patent nonsense, of course. The history of the form tells us otherwise. And writers working now explain why. In a letter to me later published in *The Reluctant Reader* Alan Garner, having first said he was not a children's writer, not a 'fantasy writer', not anything else but simply a writer, put his reasons like this:

> Yet I do want children to read the books, and especially do I want adolescents to find them. Simply, children make the best audience. Connect with a child and you really connect. Adolescence is the same only more so. [. . .] It is this thesis, that adolescence may be a form of maturity from which the adult declines, that involves me and will do so for as far ahead as I can see.

More recently Garner has refined that notion in an interview published in *Signal* 27, September 1978. But addressing the audience which you find most receptive for what you have to say is as legitimate a reason as any for exercising an art in a particular way. Writing in order to recreate your own adolescence and thus deal with it is another drive for some. Telling stories to connect one's own youth with one's children's present youth and the times they live in is the drive behind Robert Cormier's *The Chocolate War* and Robert Westall's *The Machine-Gunners*. And I get too many unsolicited manuscripts for comfort that testify to the numbers of people who *want*, for whatever reasons, to write *for* teenagers, to suppose for one moment that this is all a strange, aberrant and minority matter.

I can speak with most authority about myself. Leaving aside my work as a teacher and an editor, I can test all this out within my own experience as an author. I write *for* teenagers (as well as for adults and for children). This is not the place to explore the neurotic or experiential roots of that impulse; I'm simply noting it as an indisputable fact. My novel, *Breaktime*, resulted not from any calculated use of programmed formula, nor from deliberate invention to satisfy the postal votes on reading preferences that come from Topliner readers. In this limited and self-conscious sense, the story was not made; it happened. And while it was happening everything else to do with teenage literature was forgotten (writing a novel is too difficult a business to be thinking of things like that!). All I knew before, during, and after the event, was that I had to get the story down in this way, and that if anyone else was to read it, I would most prefer that anyone to be an adolescent. It was about the adolescent-still-in-me and it was for the adolescent-still-in-the-reader. (The book is about much else too, but leave aside the complexities for now in deference to our set topic.)

If I had wanted the book to connect with the adult-in-me, I would have done it differently. There would have been a shift in the point of view, changes in the assumed and explicit references. In short, the tone and the rhetoric of the book would have been handled another way. What those differences consist in – what makes a book *for* teenage or not – is a fascinating topic, the one we really ought to be discussing, rather than continuing the wearying argument about whether teenage books can or ought to exist. But, as I said before, we cannot explore such topics without a critical apparatus that helps us do so. The raw material for that critique is already available in great quantity. Forging it into a coherent body of work is but an academic's sinecure away. And if anything needs to be done to better the status and innovatory progress of teenage literature, that's it. For a healthy critical atmosphere stimulates writers and publishers, opens up their work to associated professionals (librarians and teachers) and thus clarifies the form and its reception.

Apart from this, the real problem about teenage literature is not whether it ought or ought not to exist – as I've said, it does and isn't about to go away – but is a problem of availability to the readers. It is not a literary problem at all, therefore, but a commercial and distributive one. Librarians still haver anxiously about what to do with the books and where to put them; teachers in secondary schools and colleges are still often lamentably ignorant of what has been produced, and in their ignorance adopt censorial prejudices against the very idea of the books. And while those two powerful bodies of buyers-on-behalf-of-teenage-readers remain so confused, publishers hesitate in identifying clearly what books of theirs belong to the category. So far, in contrast to the state of things in a number of other countries, only The Bodley Head has had the courage to nail their colours to the mast and declare what is what on their list. That is something for which writers like myself feel grateful – I would not have wanted *Breaktime* to appear unmarked on a children's list. Of the paperbackers, only Penguin, aside from the Topliner list, have tried, somewhat nervously to judge from their choice, to gather their teenage forces in the erratic Peacock list.

The aim for the future then must be, in my view, to clarify the form critically, and to tidy up and invigorate the distributive channels. The books themselves, against those presently undermining odds, continue to grow rapidly in number and to develop in nature. If teenage literature does not rule – no one would want it to – it certainly lives.

Part Two
The Books

4 The relevance of books for older children
Rosemary Sandberg

At a children's book conference a few years ago, one of our leading authors of both adult and children's books, said she did not consider there was a market for serious books for adolescents. She maintained that after the age of twelve children went straight to Ian Fleming *et al* who provided all they wanted in their reading. This was certainly food for thought. The picture, I was sure, could not be written off like that. If younger children and indeed adults too, enjoy and need a mixture of escapism and realism, of popular and quality books, of stories to be read at a sitting and those that demand more time and concentration, surely the reading pattern of those between twelve and sixteen could not be that different.

As a children's paperback editor, passionate about the role of good fiction at every age level, I was suddenly appalled lest older children were sticking with Mr Fleming and Mr Maclean, lest lasting stories did not have a place at that moment in their lives. Generalizations can be misleading, so let me say at the beginning that the avid readers will of course unearth what they need, come what may. My concern is for those who have slipped out of the serious reading habit, and for those who may never have had it. In the first case, it is vital if we believe in the value and necessity of a literate society, to boost the habit, to inject it with greater variety and intensity, and to find out whether the fault lies at the publishers' doors in not publishing appealing books, or whether the error is with the book trade in general. Whatever the reason, it is essential to make a serious bid to woo the older non-reader to give books a try, even at this comparatively late stage.

I had many lengthy discussions with older children, librarians and teachers. Sure enough, the fairly obvious pattern was confirmed: there were avid readers who were in a minotity, there were many moving directly to adult books purely for escapist reasons, and there were many who saw no relevance for books even as light entertainment. So it was certainly apparent that after the age of twelve and thirteen, the majority of children were turning away from or rejecting books. Why? Faults appear on all sides; with the publishers for seemingly not publishing the right books, with the book trade for not taking this category seriously, and with the media for not bothering to publicize the 'right' books that were published, so older children were not aware of them. Because publishing and bookselling have to be commercially viable, it is no surprise that books for a dwindling market were not being written, published, distributed, displayed or promoted.

It is interesting that the age that singled out adolescents or teenagers, is having difficulties in integrating them back into the society. The great youth syndrome proves problematic both privately in families, and publicly in schools and the community at large. The move to a reliable, mature citizen is the most difficult part of growing up. Independence and responsibility are being thrust on young people at an increasingly early age. Pressures of advertising and the press force the competitive urge in certain fields before young people have the self-confidence and maturity to think things out for themselves. A certain public role is being pushed on to them, whether they want it or not. In other words, it is no easy matter being an adolescent today.

In a recent poll in the USA, and in supportive evidence produced here, the most pressing issues concerning older children are getting on with their families – the perennial generation gap which is ever widening and the inability to communicate at the roots – and school problems and coming to terms with society. Incidentally, it is interesting that the moral issues dwelt on so heavily by the press, the three p's of pot, pill and pregnancy, are low down on the list of worries.

I firmly believe that the very intimate experience of reading must be able to help adolescents cope and understand the difficulties of any two people trying to communicate. Here is the ideal medium for the adolescent, quite privately when he doesn't have to act out a role, when he can think things out for himself, to see others going through comparable situations and to see alternative ways of behaviour and resolutions to human conflict.

Paul Zindel and Vera and Bill Cleaver have used their enormous skills as professional writers to demonstrate the difficulties of one human being getting through to another, especially when they are of different age groups. The teenage protagonists of *The Pigman* are filled with the disillusionment and dissatisfaction about home, adults and society. Zindel opens their eyes to the feelings and emotions of an old man. But they learn the hard way, through tragedy, which brings the point home with extra impact. In many books for younger children, parents remain stereotyped in the background. It is vital in books for older children that when adults appear, the author should grab the opportunity to show them as people, warts and all, so that the reader can feel sympathy for them and more readily understand their point of view. It is no help to promote the idea that communication is only possible through one's peers.

The Cleavers have a fine spectrum of characters, children and adults, who live, think, act and react in a cogent, true and diverse way. In *Grover*, the child is confounded not only at his mother's suicide, but at his father's reaction to it. Gradually Grover begins to understand that in this extreme situation his father has no blueprint of how to behave, so his wild reaction seems out of character, that his father has a range of complex emotions that cannot be explained in a quick and logical way. Strong characterization then, is all important. To distort is a waste and a lie that will diminish any book.

American authors, with their rich tradition of realist writing, from Huck Finn to Holden Caulfield, are immensely successful at creating the family scene. Virginia Hamilton in her Newbury award winning book *M. C. Higgins the Great* has succeeded better than many authors so far in showing with great compassion and understanding, the painful process of a young person coming to terms with his own adulthood and with the adults close to him. This is a difficult book, and will probably never reach the majority of those it would most likely help. But those who are encouraged to persevere will surely grow a little and understand a good deal more about themselves.

Coming to terms with school problems and with the community in general can be an even more complex and confusing business. Before them, older children glimpse the tumult of the adult world to which they are being propelled. Small wonder they resist and rebel at what they can see of it. In a time that should be filled with hope and expectation, a bewildering set of events face them that scarcely encourage aspirations: the prospect of a tedious job or even unemployment; television constantly broadcasting the horrors of agression; corruption in high places; violence and vengeance at every turn; hypocrisy and intolerance rife. What is there to encourage decent behaviour, what are the benefits of behaving like a responsible citizen when they know full well that the bad guy isn't necessarily going to lose out and the good often suffer? What motive is there for mutual trust and consideration?

Here, again, the role of books is all important. The protagonist they trust in a book, can underline the value of the young person as an individual, can offer a reason for behaving in one way as opposed to another, can restore a little hope. For an author this must be one of the most difficult tasks in the whole field of writing because there is no mid course. His/her motive must be completely honest. Any abuse will show at the seams, and the sensitive adolescent will feel once again he's being got at, and quite rightly reject the whole 'message'. Mollie Hunter, in her semi-autobiographical novel *The Sound of Chariots*, gave back the hope to her heroine that had been dashed by the injustice of her father's untimely death. Martin Ballard commends the resilience of *Dockie* in his single-mindedness and determination to escape and fight for himself, and not to follow along with the crowd. Both are rare books, and the authenticity and relevance of their themes could profoundly affect a young person coming to terms with growing up.

Although the books so far mentioned demand quite a lot of the reader, a compelling storyline runs through them all. First and foremost, books must entertain. The reader must want to turn the page to find out what happens next. No one wants to read endless sagas of something between the latch-key state and the kitchen sink. Complex characterization, relevant themes, sympathetic attitudes must be cleverly integrated into a very good and involving story, told with energy and pace. I hope that authors sympathetic to the dilemmas, panics and irritations of young people will increasingly turn their attentions to writing absorbing books for this age group. Those writers who can remember and recall their own unease will be at an advantage. The success of S. E. Hinton stems from her own experience in coming to terms with conflicts and strife among her friends when she was seventeen. Her books are entirely authentic; she doesn't moralize, she is never patronising, and she pulls it off because the reader senses her personal involvement and experience, and goes along with her opinions and suggested alternative ways of coping.

A few fine British writers have succeeded in showing a range of adolescent fears and hopes, judging from the popularity of their books in terms of sales figures: John Rowe Townsend's *The Intruder*, Alan Garner's *The Owl Service*, Bob Leeson's *The Third Class Genie*, Farrukh Dhondy's *East End at Your Feet* and *Come to Mecca* for example. But two dozen titles at most over the past six or seven years is not many.

Of course it's easier to read Ian Fleming: a quick bit of escapism, a fantasy world of spills and thrills, a high coloured, quickly evaporating dream. We need our dreams, but we desperately need reality and solutions. The school bookshops are invaluable in promoting, and bringing to the attention of the older child, the less flashy, more thought provoking books. One of the great problems, as Kaye Webb mentioned in her article in an issue of *School Bookshop News*, is publicizing children's books. Unlike the adult paperback market that thrives on what is new, children's paperbacks rely heavily on their backlist titles. TV and film tie-ins apart, a book does not usually reach high monthly sales figures until it is known about and trusted, and this sometimes takes a deal of time. Children are wary and take what is new with reluctance. Only when the ball of personal recommendation starts rolling do the sales start to climb. Alan Garner is a case in point. It took several years before he reached the backlist best-seller charts.

So nothing is going to happen over night. But with the ever growing shop window of the school bookshops displaying a wide range of books, older children will begin to experiment with new material; they'll become familiar with the title and look of a new book and will be more willing to give it a try. The book trade itself has been reluctant to recognize this midway category between children-proper and adult books. It certainly presents a tricky display problem. Adolescents are not going to go near the children's section of a bookshop, and the adult buyer is usually disinclined to place them with the adult books. But if the book is good enough, these books should ideally be displayed alongside the adult paperbacks. After all, in many public libraries, these books are on the adult shelves, and it is salutary and enjoyable for adults to read about a section of society they so often malign!

I do hope that our best writers don't share the view of the author at the conference. Books are vital to the emotional development of all children, and especially at the sensitive ages of twelve to sixteen, they can help profoundly. So please, authors, consider adolescence with all the sympathy, understanding and skill you can muster, and please teachers, persevere with these books published with such care by the publishers. Then, perhaps, we may be able to stem the tide, and make older children realize that books, serious books, are entirely relevant to their lives.

5 The vacuum and the myth
Robert Westall

Let me tell you about the daughter of a friend of mine, whom I'll call Jane Short. Jane's fourteen; friendly, pretty and warmly attached to her parents, but socially timid, especially for the London commuter-belt comprehensive she attends.

The school runs an evening youth club. There was going to be a disco. A friend finally persuaded Jane to go.

In the first half-hour she was standing in the corner of the hall when, to her horror, she heard the DJ announce that Jane Short had requested a record for one particular boy. She was shattered. She hardly knew the boy, didn't even like him. Everyone was staring at her, thinking her pushy. Some unknown person had played a very dirty trick on her.

Worse followed. The boy's girlfriend crossed the hall, beside herself with jealousy. She would wait outside to get Jane. She would get her at school the next day as well. Not just the girlfriend, but all the girlfriend's girlfriends in all the days to come.

Worse still, not one of Jane's so-called friends stood by her; not even the dubious character who had asked her to the disco in the first place.

Jane had to walk home alone in the dark. After massive support from her calm and steady mother, she somehow got herself to school next day. Nothing happened, physically, but Jane has never been back to the youth club and she has rather given up believing in friendship. She had sampled the vacuum where the young live now; a vacuum without rules, left by the retreat of the middle-aged.

To see how much this vacuum has grown, we must look at how Jane's grandmother must have attended her first dance. Not at fourteen, but a much more mature seventeen. The hall would have been half-full of authoritarian supportive adults. The worst that could have happened to Jane's grandmother was that she might have had to sit out the dance as a wallflower. Humiliating, but not so bad as having your whole social and work-scene blow up in your face, without warning, and not through any fault of your own. Leaving a landscape as bleak and threatening as midnight Manhattan. A landscape without rules, even teenage rules.

As a schoolmaster, I see this landscape daily. Thirty years ago, as a schoolboy, I found the rules clear enough. Never split on another boy to the teacher. Or you got thumped. And knew you deserved it.

Today, boys split on each other daily, for a cheap laugh.

In my day, boys fought one to one. When one got knocked down and stayed down, that was the end of it. Now it is more often five or ten to one. And if you get knocked down, don't stay down, or someone might be tempted to put the boot in.

In my day, you gave allegiance to a gang, and the gang protected you. Same as in Tom Brown's schooldays.

Today, you stand up for no one, and no one stands up for you. It is Bully Flashman's paradise. Schoolboy honour? I haven't heard the phrase in years. Because schoolboy honour was no more and no less than the rules the gangs lived by, and in schools, we no longer give gangs a chance to form.

Of course, 'gang' has become a dirty word, implying violence and hooliganism. That wasn't so forty years ago, when 'Our Gang' was a beloved comic-strip. For the authors of 'Our Gang' knew what modern educationists have forgotten – that gangs are simply the basic social structure boys (and perhaps girls) form, *when they are allowed to*. But the formation of gangs (and therefore rules) requires stability and continuity. The kind given by boys living together as a form, in a recognized form-room, in charge of a recognized form-master . . . Having most of their lessons together as a form.

This was still important to boys ten years ago. I knew a second-form who simply gave up working. When their sensitive form-master asked them why, they said they knew they were going to be split up after the Christmas exams and restreamed. They said 'We've spent a whole year working out who's top-dog in this form, and who's bottom, and who belongs to which gang. Now it will be all to do again, and we haven't the heart.' Informed they were not to be split up, they immediately returned to normal working. This need for hierarchy is shared by all the animal kingdom. Put three strange horses in a field, and they will spend the first few hours working out their pecking order.

But in the last ten years of educational experiment, via unstreaming and banding, setting in subjects and grouping in houses, we have practically destroyed the form structure. Last year, my son did not have one single lesson together with the whole of his form. At home, he has a gang, and friends he can rely on; at school, no gang and no friends to rely on. So comes the stage of alienation where a boy can be punched in the stomach and lie on the ground till he recovers, while hundreds pass by uncaring. Why should they care? He is not in their gang; he is not their friend.

In such a gangless unstructured situation, the vacuum grows. As schoolboys, we loved hot classroom debates, arguing with masters and testing adult wisdom. Now I find boys will not open their mouths. Not for fear of the teacher, but for fear of what their contemporaries will make of any rash statement, afterwards. One first-former I knew admitted that he missed his dead father. Even now, in the sixth, he suffers from taunts of 'Rent-a-Dad, Rent-a-Dad'.

At home, too, the vacuum grows. The older I get, the more I become aware that my adolescent world-view was built up over many evenings at home, pretending to read a book, but really listening to my parents talking to each other. Evenings of what we would now regard as tedium and boredom. Such a world-view had its faults; it was narrow and parochial. But what is sound and narrow can be built on later. At least my parents' world-view was of a piece, graspable.

Now we have the goggle-box. To me, the worst thing about the goggle-box is that it presents a series of vivid, disturbing, disconnected fragments that can never hang together. How can any child, unaided, put together a world-view from a Kojak episode, a nature-film about the Wild Dogs of Africa, and a documentary on Hong-Kong prostitutes? It takes *me* all my time. The best thing I do for my son is to watch telly with him, exchanging loud and heated commentary while the programmes are in progress (much to the annoyance of my wife).

But what of children who view alone, and see the battered face of a man murdered in Northern Ireland suddenly flashed, without warning, on the screen? Do they despair of ever making a world-view that fits together? Do they despairingly settle for a life of disconnected fragments that are therefore meaningless? Like the Dutch teenager Petra who wrote,

At home they would never understand anything . . . people only care for external appearances – whether you passed your exams, get enough sleep. You rarely find anyone fundamentally interested in others.

I am alone. Suddenly you are supposed to solve all your own problems; to face what only a grownup can face.

I don't belong anywhere. I am frightened to see all the things that are going on in the world; now all these problems fall on me. I feel I ought to do something – since the adults won't. But I am helpless; I don't know where to start. I feel like an animal, just vegetating. Then it seems that my life and life itself is without meaning.

This is the teenage vacuum. Increasingly abandoned by adult authority; their own hierarchies unwittingly destroyed; increasingly cut off from meaningful dialogue with helpful adults; increasingly exposed to the fragmented disasters of the media, the young wander increasingly lost. One of their reactions is to shrink away, like Petra. Another is the nihilistic vandalism of the football special.

I do not wish to overstate my case; many parents and teachers are fighting noble and successful rearguard actions. Nevertheless, this is the way the tide is setting; this is the landscape into which the writer of teenage novels must now venture.

I say 'teenage novels' and not 'children's books'. I am not concerned with the under-twelves. They are, in a way, still warmly encapsulated in the gentleness of home and primary school. My readership starts at the point when, soon after reaching secondary school, the adolescent realizes he must protect his own parents from harsher facts of adolescent life. It is then he becomes alone.

Children's books have different aims: broadening vocabulary, widening the imagination, simply inculcating the habit of reading. The teenage novel must enter what I might term 'the battle of the myths'.

I do not mean simply Greek or Norse myths. Cinderella is a myth. By myth, I mean a story that blasts a channel in your mind, down which future experience may flow. Cinderella teaches us that no matter how downtrodden you are, however wretched the circumstances you are reduced to, you need make no efforts to help yourself. If you wait long enough, some magic friend will leap to your aid and transform your life into a paradise. Compulsive gamblers are believers in the Cinderella myth. Perhaps we're all Cinderellas now. Our Ugly Sisters, France and Germany, have gone to the European Ball. We wait for North Sea Oil to turn our pumpkin into a golden coach . . .

Brer Rabbit is a much more positive kind of myth. He has a high survival-value. No matter how bad your situation, keep and use your wits, and you'll come out on top. He teaches lateral-thinking better than Edward de Bono. Perhaps the Israelis who raided Entebbe had had a surfeit of Brer Rabbit, and been entirely deprived of Cinderella.

But viewed from another angle (the Buddhist angle, or the Quaker angle) Brer Rabbit sums up all that is worst in Western Europeans: materialistic, on the make, solving everything by offensive action, wily rather than wise. Myths can be two-edged things.

I have no more room to analyse them here; you can do it for yourself. What I want to point out is that two factors are at work now, destroying the store of myths that we have lived by for centuries. One destroyer is the television advert, which picks up myths then cheapens and destroys them. The old myth of the small boy's nourishing relationship with a wise grandfather figure is butchered to make a Hovis advert.

The other destroyer is what I can only term the Monty Python Gang. I too thought they were *very* funny, until I saw what they were up to. It is, perhaps, not *too* destructive to stand up the figure of King Arthur as an aunt-sally to throw cow-dung at; though some of our best literature is based on the Arthurian myths; and how many children will turn away automatically from books about Arthur, now they have been enlightened that he's simply a dung-splattered buffoon? And wouldn't the dung-treatment be equally funny applied to Jesus running away in a silly nightshirt or to Buddha talking like a Peter Sellers Indian Doctor? Switched into the creative vein of Monty-Pythonism, I can imagine terrible things happening to Gandhi (bandy-legged), Schweitzer (hand up African ladies' skirts), Bertrand Russell (who we now learn was invalidated as a philosopher because he was a philanderer with bad breath). Nothing is safe from Monty-Pythonism. But when the laughing stops, what have we got left to live by?

Perhaps we have to create new myths. If so, I can think of no one better qualified than those I shall call the teenagers' novelists. I have read a lot of teenage novels recently, and I have read few without integrity and a desire to offer something good. Perhaps this is because no one can hope to become rich writing them. Many are written by parents, *as parents* – the equivalent of my father telling me tales of what he got up to as a lad, on those so-called evenings of tedium long ago. *Watership Down* began with Richard Adams telling his daughters tales to while away long car-journeys. Hazel and El-Ahrairah are superior versions of Brer Rabbit – Brer Rabbit with a spiritual dimension added. It would be easy to run off into a long list of helpful myths found in teenage novels. I will content myself with one – the teenage girl whom Jill Paton Walsh turns into a grand-mother with one tremendous *coup de main* in her novel *Unleaving*. I cannot think of a nobler blow to strike, in these days when it is increasingly the habit of social workers and doctors to refer to old people (and especially old people in homes) as 'moggies'. 'Moggies' is a comic-cruel word, implying that the old do not suffer so much pain, have not such valid desires as the young and middle-aged. It is good to be reminded that there is a 'moggie' within us all . . .

The worst thing about today's teenage novels is that *vis-à-vis* the media, and the Monty Pythonists, they are small fish with very small teeth. (*Watership Down* is the honourable exception.) I was very content sitting on my little *Machine-gunners* anthill (6,000 hardback English sales; American, French and Japanese rights sold) until I learnt that the Monty Python Mob regard 40,000 hardback sales as a *failure*. Thus I was brought to a true picture of my own futility and impotence to help. The teenage novelists, if they are to redress that balance at all, must grow much bigger teeth.

What teeth? The first I might term the Battle of the First Two Pages. I have watched children in libraries, working along the shelves. They pick up a book, read the first page, perhaps skim the second, then put it back on the shelf. (Or in tougher schools they may drop it on the floor, where it becomes a football and dies quickly.) We must get our bite in and ruffle the surface of a child's indifference before the end of page one. This is not cheap, sensational or journalistic. In Alan Garner's *The Owl Service* the bite (the myster-ious noise in the ceiling) goes in at the bottom of page one, and that book won the Carnegie award. It is a trait Garner shares with the scriptwriter of 'Kojak' and none the worse for that. If you can't beat them, join them.

The second tooth I shall call 'From the Horse's Mouth'. Reality has a wry, salt, enigmatic, idiosyncratic flavour that no mere invention can ever equal, and that all of us, including children, instantly recognize and are hooked-on. Let me compare two novels on the same topic, Boadicea's rebellion. Stephanie Plowman's *To Spare the Conquered* is a very reasonable read – much used in schools. It impresses – until you compare it with George Shipway's *Imperial Governor*. For Shipway had the advantage of experiencing the military conqueror's dilemmas as an officer in the Indian Army. He doesn't have to invent – merely to transpose real experience.

Shipway's novel is all the better because the hero, Paulinus, reels from crisis to crisis – the hard knobs of real life hem him in on every side. He has no time for the histrionic gesture – he is fighting for his life, and the reader fights with him every inch of the way. This is my third tooth – involving the reader in real dilemmas. Perhaps the thought is best expressed by Stephen Vincenszay, in his novel *In Praise of Older Women*:

> A novel becomes life-like not by describing life, but by putting the reader in a 'live' situation, in which he is compelled to exercise his judgment, guess at the meaning of an action or a gesture, and try to estimate character with no more clues than he would have in reality.

The best moment for me in writing *The Machine-gunners* was when my son Christopher leapt up shouting 'Chas is a fool – he should have done this – he should have done that'. In other words, he was taking the hero's dilemmas on himself, and *thinking of his own way of solving them*. Children have, thank God, long since rejected moral preaching – but they still greatly enjoy moral exercise.

But to get this effect, a teenage novel must allow its hero (or heroine) real power. Power to change their own lives – or to ruin the lives of others. This is what the machine-gun represents in *The Machine-gunners*. And to give such power to children is not unrealistic – I have known children who broke up their parents' marriages, children who drove teachers into a nervous breakdown.

That is why I dislike teenage novels in which children are helpless bystanders or merely little helpers. I do not want children to be faced with the inner dilemmas of Kaiser Bill's Batman. I want them to be faced with the dilemmas of Kaiser Bill himself.

The last tooth sounds a truism. Tell children about things they are interested in. One day last summer, I found Christopher, my son, with his head buried in a fat adult book. It stayed buried in that book for four whole days. The telly lay silent; he had to be dragged to meals. I thought he was ill – I kept on poking him to make sure he was still alive.

The book was Herman Wouk's *The Caine Mutiny*. It concerns a mutiny aboard an American destroyer in World War II. Although it contains scenes of violence, it is mild compared with say 'Starsky and Hutch'. I was baffled. And then I realized. It was about *gangs* – about a young sprog trying to find his place in a gang, then about the overthrow of the gang-leader. If the gang are adult, have a destoyer to play with, and are fighting the Japs so much the better. But it wasn't the heart of it, for Christopher finds Douglas Reeman's books of naval warfare repetitive and, in his own word 'clichaic'. Violence is not the interest – ganglife, the old abiding social structure, is the interest.

And, on looking around, I find this interest in the gangs holds true. Kojak has his gang (and gained the ascendancy over Harry O, who is a loner); Hazel has his gang in *Watership Down*; Jim Hawkins and Long John Silver have their gangs in *Treasure Island* (and treat each other with the respect that gang-leaders deserve).

That is why *The Machine-gunners* is about a gang; it hopes to serve a hunger for social-structure in the young which, at the moment, we are very far from meeting.

6 Words into life
Paul Zindel

I have been invited to share a few words with you about what's on my mind these days, and I find those few words fall into two categories: (a) Is there really any such animal as a novel for young adults? and (b) if there is, what should we do with it? Well, there is such an animal and we should use it to disimprison our youth.

First I must describe the animal to you as I see it:

It is SCHOOL ORIENTED. Teenagers go to school, and quite naturally are stimulated by academic references and environments in their fiction. In *The Pigman* much of my international fan mail tells of the delight in finding its hero set off a firecracker in the boys' bathroom. Also young readers love to discover that other school cafeterias exist which serve soup tasting like boiled sneakers. And they absolutely adore hyperbole when applied to teachers and librarians, whether it's the humour of nicknaming one 'The Cricket' or the pathos of one who kept her dying mother in a bed in the living room.

Young people like stories in which the PARENTS HAVE SMALL ROLES. There are exceptions to all these points but let's not quibble. The teen years are the time to break away and define one's Self, and a young reader will sniff suspiciously if he comes across too many paragraphs devoted to how omnipotently competent and deliriously happy the adults are – particularly because he knows there are now about eight thousand self-help books on the market for these older astute folk. In *My Darling, My Hamburger* I deliberately kept the parents in the background because that was the way the story unfolded in real life. Liz, who goes to get an abortion, really couldn't turn to her mother or father because they were (you might as well know here although it isn't in the book) both over six feet tall, loud, domineering, and surrounded their children with the largest appliances in the world including a General Electric toaster which could pop out eight slices at a clip.

Young people love books written in the FIRST PERSON. This point of view demands that every word of the book be as a kid would see and say it. In my *Confessions of a Teenage Baboon* I found the technique particularly successful because it allowed me to deal with the threats to a boy's sexuality without rapaciously ripping into some of the more ghastly adult opinions I have about that subject – opinions which would bore the pants off any kid. My young narrator never once had to tiptoe through the complexities of transvestism and sexual preference and all those other euphemisms which fairly well keep the lid on what is basically a crippling script. (Kindly direct all mail on the last remarks to A. Bryant, Miami, Florida – or the North African Tourist Board.)

DELICIOUS LANGUAGE is also important; language which gives the appearance of being contemporary but not so trendy that it will date in ten years. Oxymorons are worshipped here, second only to phrases which combine the sublime with the unexpectedly absurd – for example, a raccoon sandwich. I took my lead here from an article in *The New York Times* on stories written and published by teenagers themselves. One girl called her story 'She Was Nice To Mice'. A boy called his story 'The Cockroach of the 86th Street Crosstown Bus'. Why should adults writing for the young adult be any less creative? Of course, I test-market my titles with the kids. My newest book *The Undertaker's Gone Bananas* was originally called *The Mortician's Gone Nuts*, but when I went into classrooms for advice the pupils asked me 'What's a mortician?' I queried, 'Do you know what an undertaker is?' They all said, 'Oh, yes!' Then I quizzed them on their favourite word for insane and discovered it was the same word that was popular when I was in school thirty years ago. Any word that's around for thirty years is no longer slang except for purists badly in need of a high colonic.

Kids love romance. ROMANCE! No explanation necessary except that it's hard to come by at any age.

HONESTY. H. L. Menchen said 'Youth, though it may lack knowledge, is certainly not devoid of intelligence. It can see through shams with a sharp and terrible eye.' If he didn't say it, he said something like it. In *I Never Loved Your Mind* I had to use a few invectives because that was how those kids spoke. And Yvette, the earth-girl had to go off and leave Dewey the Innocent, and . . . oh, I'm just going to stop this paragraph right here because I think I'm beginning to stretch things a bit just to get in the name of every one of my books. More succinctly, kids like a pancake called a pancake.

And MISCHIEF – this is the one quality I find adults tend to phase out and enjoy more by proxy or through ribald humoresques told by barbers, and women's movement magazines. Mischief is, of course, a form of play, sometimes risky play. In all of my books I make certain the young reader gets his share of off-stage and on-stage mad kids doing things like dropping balloons filled with water from roofs or getting dressed up in costumes for various effects; clerical garb is a favourite. Offering candies at a party and then telling the munchers that they really aren't chocolate-covered Rice Krispies, but indeed ants – runs a close second. TRANSITIONAL PICTURES are greatly appreciated and I used them abundantly in *The Pigman* – a relief from cold hard print, which actually is the way kids write. *Literary graffiti* – they love to put doodles and arrows and other graphics on their compositions and epistles. Letters in *italics* are even appreciated, and considering the escalation of printing costs its a good thing I chose only such relief for *Pardon Me, You're Stepping On My Eyeball*. Thanks to the letters connected to the character of Marsh Mellow, that book is the most italicized tome in history.

Needless to say, young adults like ACTION AND SUSPENSE. This was made somewhat clear to me when I was a high school sophomore and our English teacher, Miss Kalling, who was a Shakespearean scholar, threatened to jump out the third floor classroom window and land head-first on the cement below. We, the students, were being particularly inattentive while she was dramatizing one of the more provocative speeches from *All's Well that Ends Well*, when she screamed and rushed to the window, throwing it open and swinging her not terribly unattractive legs over the ledge. 'Stop this or I'll jump!' she ordered, seated, prepared to fly. The class in unison responded swiftly: 'Jump!' A certain Mr Stuart, then the Dean of Boys (he's dead now), darted in the front door and secured Miss Kalling before she could follow through with her temptation and one could sense the disappointment of the youngsters in the room.

What is most vital is that a book for young adults should be SHORT. Short books for short book reports! This may appear to be bathos of a sort, but it is not.

Herewith are halted the ten articulations of the animal known as a novel for young adults. There is probably an eleventh implied in this letter from Kathie Willhite of Tulsa, Oklahoma: *To Mr Paul Zindel* –

When you feel something very deeply it is often difficult to say exactly what is rattling around in your brain. 'Ah ha!' you say, 'An insane teenager has written to me!' Not far off base really. I just finished *Pardon Me, You're Stepping on my Eyeball*. It pulled part of me out and I want to finish this letter before that part of me goes back in. I am still not quite coherent and usually that means I'm at my best. I wanted to cry so bad that it hurt. Something in me refused to let go and I couldn't. I know a person like Marsh Mellow who hides sometimes from reality and I think that is what held in the tears. I cried too many times for him and I just didn't have any left for Marsh. I don't know why and I won't hazard a guess but I am almost afraid to read any of your other books. I cannot see what makes a person write such a book but it had a part of everyone in it and I can't tell which one was me. I'm moved and I'm almost speechless and I want you to know that.

I think what this girl was telling me was that she understood the emotional investment from my remembered youth and my selfish insistence that each story I write must solve a problem for *me*!

I know how good a book is from the amount of crying I do as I type the last line. If I type the final line and I *don't* cry I know there's something dishonest about the book's content. For that reason I always type the last line while slicing onions. I also use life models. I call them 'Inspirational Homunculi'.

Now on to how these young adult books should be used to improve the lives of our youth. A book is created by a writer who observes life and then freezes it into words. I think here's where we really need the school experience and the inspired teacher and librarian. It's all very nice that a kid can have a good read on his own. It's all very pleasant if a class, miraculously rare, can have their fun at the same time, too. But what I find most exciting is when the words of the book are turned back into life. A book is a departure point from which kids can take a page, a written event – and turn it into an experience. The actual experience captured in the book is not half as important as a kid *himself* being able to speak out in a class and to say:

Hey, I understand what these words say, that John Conlan sat across from his girlfriend and they had secrets to share over a candlelit dinner they concocted; And Hey, I think I would have done something else if I was left alone in a house with a girl like that. I would have behaved differently here and the same as John at another point; And Hey, this event reminds me of the time I was alone with a girl in a cemetery and we told each other we heard footsteps and thought we saw a hand reach out of a grave!

What I'm trying to say is that a young adult book in particular offers a grand opportunity to take full advantage of word and phrase configurations as a take-off point from which a boy and girl can enter into the *performance* of life. Jung knew a single alien letter from an unknown alphabet was enough to trigger endless thoughts in the human mind. Imagine the power of a whole book in the hands of a teacher and class. A paragraph would be enough to provoke a balance between the sending and receiving which must occur in the learning process. Right now in America we are just beginning to dream of turning away from fact bombardment and opening up our ears to listen to the kids. So many of our pupils are breathtakingly ignorant, and I mean that in the loftiest sense of the word. The rather shocking and horrible part of having created so many dummies is that, precisely as stated, they were *created*. We were so busy sending information we never let the kids speak up for themselves. The scenario went as follows: a lot of kids were made to feel they were not very worthy. The villains were the schools, teachers, parents, peers, and several mogul-dominated electronic devices. Kids who were not fed back a positive image of themselves, mainly due to a lack of opportunity to express themselves, did one of three things: they became as silent as wallpaper; they developed into neurotics floundering in psychosomatic ills; or they committed acts of violence in proportion to the acts of neglect; the refusals to let them contribute or *perform*. There is that word again. So many children in schools are denied expressing their experiences, and hearing of the experiences of others. So many never had a chance to think of goals, success paths, or, simply, opportunities to practise showing their emotions.

Gaining confidence and belief that one *could* speak to groups were never our recent priorities for the young. There was little chance to

47

learn that one had a right to talk, or how to vitalize expression, or how to give appreciation to others for sharing. Books in schools could have been used to help each pupil crash through his or her shell of self-consciousness – or for the garrulous few, to help them shut up once in a while. Almost all speech therapists agree the biggest problem they have in improving a person's speech is to get a person to open his mouth. Our schools have been for open books and closed mouths. To hell with that. Let's let our kids lift their books *and* their voices. Maybe, just maybe, the young will no longer hate reading, school, and the world as much. Words should at every age mean a better life for the reader.

7 On back-tracking
Jill Paton Walsh

I am in a drawing-room. A spacious pleasant room, with the windows giving glimpses of the sea. But all I can see is sky, because I am very low down in the room; the sills are above my head. Perhaps I am, even then, lying on the floor, reading, a posture I like best even now. There is a clock in the room, ticking steadily. I like the room, I like the clock, but usually I hear the clock only when I am alone. Now the room has adults in it, sitting in the fireside chairs, without speaking. They are waiting. Their silence breaks my thread of thought as their talk could never have done. The clock begins to strike, with a little whirring sound as it gathers itself for the effort. In the moment between the whirr and the first ding my grandfather gets up and puts on the radio. The radio emits Big Ben striking six, totally upstaging the quiet little strike of the drawing-room clock.

They are all listening to the news. I understand nothing, nothing. France. The news is about the British army in France. The wordless emotion in the room weighs me down, presses me down, crushing the breath out of me. There is a map over the mantle shelf. My grandfather moves some pins on the map. He sits down. They all look at the map, at each other. An uncle begins to speak. My grandmother shushes him, inclines her head towards me to remind him. I am suddenly terrified; I must *understand* this – there is something I have to know, as one has, if one walks the rock pools, to know about the rising tide. Why are we fighting anyway? what are we trying to stop him doing?

'Grandpa?' I say, pulling gently at his trouser turnup. 'What will happen if Hitler wins?'

He tells me gruffly, gently, but with immense force, his whole strength of mind and years in his answer –

'He *won't* win!'

Years later I am in angry conflict with my father. I say we too are war criminals, we should not have used the atom bomb. Yes, I know

49

my argument would outlaw the bombing of Dresden too, yes I think it was wicked to bomb Dresden as we did . . . my father says to me wearily, 'Anyone can say that now. You have to remember we didn't know who was going to win.' And I know he is wrong. I know that knowing who was going to win was somehow part of being what I in my callow youth would have called rightmindedness; it has taken me another twenty years to remember how I knew. I should have said to my father 'Grandpa knew'.

My father would have said, 'Oh, well, he would!'

Of course one cannot spend one's adult life, one's prime energies writing for children without wondering from time to time why one does it, even if one were not always being asked. Defending it, advocating its sufficient importance and seriousness as a thing to do seems inseparable from doing it. I am not tired of writing for young readers, but I am very tired of defending it. I have so often explained that I am not an educationalist, that I hope my writing is good rather than does good; that I am not a therapist, that I think that literature should take the reader out of himself, herself into other and unlike selves, not offer a prefabricated self-identification; that I get asked for a book about a kid with spina-bifida in a slum in Darlington in adult, middle-class accents, but the kids in Darlington say 'Have you ever written about a treasure island?' or 'Will you write a book about a pony next?' All this I have said and written so often that I feel it will dry the ribbon and jam the keys if I write it all down again. I would like to approach the question in a different way.

C. S. Lewis said, 'I have been a child'. And though that is both obvious and true of us all, it rings in my ears like a profound statement of character. Nine tenths of those who speak of *children* in the context of what books they should have, think of children as a special kind of others; those who write the books tend to think of *childhood* and to regard childhood as an epoch of the self. Of course this gives rise to some amusing sidelights on human nature. Those who work with children and struggle to educate them tend to see them in terms of their shortfall from adult estate, in terms of their limitations. They expect the implied reader in a children's book to be a more or less incapable soul for whom things must be cut down. A children's book in which the author's voice addresses the readers as equals produces, only too often, agitation about the vocabulary, fog-index of the sentence structure, print size, etc., etc., or even a curious kind of adult pulling of rank – 'That's not a children's book – I quite enjoyed it myself!' I once heard.

On the other hand, the writer who is working for the child he remembers himself to have been can usually be seen working for an exceptionally sensitive, fresh intelligence, whose inexperience is a shining Blakean innocence, who is misunderstood and under-estimated by the world around him. He sees his reader not in terms of present limitations, but in terms of boundless possibilities.

Each and either of these views of childhood is open to suspicion – specifically the suspicion that it is entertained in order to bolster someone's self-esteem. And yet, however rosy a view an adult takes of the child he used to be, however self-flattering and untypical that child may seem to be to someone knowing a fair sample of children from the outside, as it were, yet it is quite something, isn't it, for an adult to be *able* to remember the child he once was. How many people ever *would* say 'I have been a child?'

Isn't it true, and very odd, that most adults have forgotten? Most of us can remember, of course, odd incidents, though even these are more often remembered, I think, in our parents' fond retellings than directly; but to remember what it felt like to be a child, is rare, I think. Most people can remember themselves back into adolescence; that is when they first struck out for themselves, made choices, started to become who they are. Ask for the story of their life, and it will skither rapidly over childhood, and begin somewhere in the mid-teens. Indeed the prevailing amnesia about childhood is so frequent a consequence of maturity it can even seem like a pre-condition of it, as it does in that famous remark 'When I was a child, I spake as a child, I understood as a child, I thought as a child, but when I became a man I put away childish things'. The comparison of a child's vision with seeing through a glass darkly, which immediately follows, proves to my satisfaction that the saint was afflicted with the general amnesia I am talking about; for childhood vision, at least as remembered by me has an extreme exactitude, and painful clarity, like pictures projected too brightly on a screen. Recalling time past I am compelled into the present tense.

For a long time I thought it was this which had made me a children's writer.

I think now that that is too superficial a view. For although it is true, I am sure, that only those who can remember childhood are likely to be able to write well for children (a fact which is as clearly proved in bad writing for the young as in good) yet there is another, antecedent question, which is what *makes* some adults remember childhood so clearly when most forget? My theory is that each one of us tends to regard as the most important epoch in life that epoch in which there was first a crisis in our own lives. For each of us the definition of self begins with differences from others, and we can remember our own history back to what we see as its origin. If I am right, then a person to whom nothing of shattering impact happened until they were a young adult will tend to have mostly forgotten childhood, and to regard children as very half-formed people. If they become writers their books will be about young adults. A person whose life followed a very conventional course until middle age, and then met crisis will, on becoming a writer, tend to put middle age crisis in the centre of the stage. And a person to whom things happened in childhood will tend to remember that far back, and write about childhood, if they write. Charles Dickens, his young soul deeply seared by the blacking-factory, wrote about the child-hoods of his characters, and for adult readers. He assumed that childhood was interesting to adults, a natural enough assumption which has fallen from favour these days so that writing about children and writing for them has become fudged into the same thing. That has the odd result occasionally of leading people to offer children spectacularly 'unsuitable' books, just because they have child protagonists. *The Turn of The Screw*, *The Lord of the Flies*, *High Wind in Jamaica*, and the re-issue for children of Nina Bawden's *Devil by the Sea* spring to mind.

It is, I think, the attraction of childhood as a *subject* that makes many children's writers; though of course a person who believes in the interest and importance of childhood as a subject is likely also to think of children as an important audience. They are a deeply prob-lematic audience, for the simple reason that nobody can reach them without the mediation of adults – not with a hardback in any circumstances, and even with a paperback very seldom. There is therefore a kind of obstacle race to be run; one must get past those intervening adults. Not, of course, without touching them; no worse atmosphere could be created for a book than that of boredom or contempt on the part of those who have to hand it on. Adults are part of the audience for children's books, and must be catered for. Not that that in itself is any problem; it was the mainstream tradition of the novel to be written for family consumption, and families contain all age groups. Dickens wrote for families; Thackeray had to and complained of it; modern children's writers who feel not more confined by their audience than Dickens and Thackeray were by theirs have little to fret about.

Speaking for myself I find the task of writing for a mixed audience technically very exacting, technically fascinating, and I do not expect to come to the end of my interest in it as long as I can sit up and type. The fascination comes from the difficulty, and the difficulty lies in getting through to the adult part of the audience with such appeal that they will be eager to pass the book on to the children they deal with, at the same time making sure that when the book arrives at a child there will be something in it for that child to enjoy. And I do not just mean some little easy bits . . . no writer who has read both his or her reviews (written by adults) and his or her fan mail (written with touching generosity by children themselves) could believe for a moment that the hard and subtle aspects of a book are liked by adults and the obvious aspects by children. More like the reverse!

The mixed audience is difficult, but it can be managed. The impossible audience is of adults who absolutely will not play, and too often that is the audience for which the children's writer is asked to write. What do I mean by that? I mean the adults who read insisting that they read not for themselves, but for children conceived of as different from adults; *unlike* beings whose requirements are not to be hooked, moved, thrilled, touched or amused, but consist of needs for limited vocabularies, subjects to compete with the box, coarse-grained simple statements, moral exhortation . . . the audience you cannot write for is the one that insists on regarding what you write as a tool for doing things to other people with – for educating young minds, correcting attitudes, spreading righteousness or whatever. Such people never conceive of themselves as being in need of the medicine they seek to administer; what writer was ever asked for a book to make the adult interlocutor less sexist or racist or class-biased? In effect they are holding themselves *outside* the circle, outside the audience for the book. Any book they approve of is likely to be mistrusted by the child when he gets it, because children, like everyone else, dislike being 'got at' – manipulated on the sly. Lessons should be openly lessons – books should be real books. Just cast your mind back to how *you* felt as a child!

And there's the nub of it. Can you cast your mind back that far? Are you still, among other people, the child you once were? If you are, you are part of the ideal and immortal audience for children's books, or any books come to that. If you are not then a real openness to children's books may help you track yourself back, as at the opening of this article I was tracking back my views of war to an origin in a very young self indeed.

Track ourselves back, and find, what? True common ground with the children in our lives, real pleasure in children's books, those certainly – and maybe something better still. For a greater and holier man than the saint quoted above said that unless we could become as little children we should not enter the kingdom of heaven; and that, I suspect, contains a profound psychological truth, even if heaven for you is not beyond the skies nor yet a primaeval garden, but the calm and mature enjoyment of the real world and the other people in it, young and old.

8 The pleasure and perils of writing young adult novels

Robert Cormier

The telephone rang late one afternoon in January. The voice asked: 'Is this the Hertz residence?' The voice was female and young – possibly a teenager.

'No,' I replied. And then remembered. 'Are you calling Amy Hertz?' Hesitation, then: 'Yes.'

I should have known. 'She's not here at the moment,' I said.

'Oh'. Then quickly: 'Thank you'. She hung up, the dial tone punctuating our brief conversation.

This had happened before, the calls always taking me by surprise although I should be prepared for them by now. The callers, always young, and male as often as female, keep the conversations short, making only the briefest of contacts. It's as if they merely want to establish Amy Hertz's identity, to confirm their suspicion that the number they're calling is an actual number and might have been – or is now – Amy's. Why do they hang up so quickly? Maybe because for one stunning moment, fiction becomes fused with reality, and they find themselves caught in a strange, never-never land.

To anyone who has not read my novel, *I Am The Cheese*, the foregoing may seem at best mysterious and at worst pointless. The fact is that Amy Hertz is a character in the novel. The novel's protagonist Adam Farmer, tries to call her on the telephone several times. For the sake of verisimilitude, I wanted to use an actual number with an actual area code. My wife suggested that I use our own number. Why not? As a result, we have had, oh, a dozen or so ghostly phone calls over the months, several of them long distance (but none person-to-person) from people trying to contact Amy Hertz, or at least asking for her.

The telephone also played a role in the aftermath of the publication of *The Chocolate War*, a novel of mine which preceded *I Am The Cheese*. The call came more than a year ago, late on a Friday morning.

A youthful voice, this time male. He gave his name and said he was calling from a high school in South Carolina. (I live in Massachusetts, about 1,000 miles away.) He said his class had been reading and discussing *The Chocolate War* and was deadlocked in a disagreement. To solve the problem, he and his classmates had been given permission by their teacher to call me. How had they tracked me down? The novel's jacket noted that I was employed by a Massachusetts newspaper. (I had since left the newspaper to devote myself full time to writing.) They called the newspaper and the switchboard operator gave them my home number. Getting down to business, the student said he was calling specifically because some members of the class believed that Jerry Renault, the protagonist, had died at the end of the novel while others in the class believed he did not die. (The novel ends as Jerry is being carried off to the hospital in an ambulance and it begins with the words, 'They murdered him,' meaning Jerry.) The students wanted to know: was Jerry symbolically murdered or did he actually die? I explained that in the fictional world of *The Chocolate War*, Jerry did not literally die, that in fact he was a presence (the word *presence* was chosen carefully) in a sequel I had begun to write. The boy whooped with delight. 'Great,' he said, 'I figured he was alive at the end.' Then he asked me to repeat the information to another student, presumably from the opposition. I told him I'd be glad to and that I would go one step further. I'd send along a letter, confirming it all, with full explanations.

And then there was the letter from the thirteen-year-old girl who said she had just finished reading *I Am The Cheese*. Twice. 'I do not understand some things about the book. I loved it, though,' she wrote. There followed a list of questions about aspects of the book I had left purposely ambiguous. She continued: 'I feel this book has done something to me. I do not know yet what, but I have told my friends to read it . . .' She ended the letter: 'Sincerely, your friend.' And her signature.

What to make of all this – the telephone calls, and the letter from the girl which more or less echoes the sentiments of countless letters I've received? Before trying to answer that question, let me say at the outset that I have never regarded myself as a 'young adult' author although both *The Chocolate War* and *I Am The Cheese* as well as my latest novel, *After The First Death*, have been published as 'young adult' novels.

Although I had been aware of writers who published books for children – picture books with big type or the Tom Swift kind of thing – I did not know that 'young adult' authors actually existed until I was told, upon acceptance of *The Chocolate War* for publication, that it would be marketed for the YA audience. ('What does YA mean?' I asked.) I had written three earlier novels which had escaped labelling. Their major characters were: a man dying of cancer; a thirty-eight-year-old widow faced with a moral problem; and a seventy-year-old man running away from what used to be known as the 'poor house'. My fourth novel, *The Chocolate War*, dealt with a fourteen-year-old boy in a critical school situation. I wrote the novel with all the care and passion with which I'd written the others, not conscious of addressing a particular audience but intent on creating believable characters in a believable world.

Suddenly, on publication, I was hailed as a new 'young adult' novelist. I thought: what's happening here? I wasn't described as an 'old man' novelist when I wrote about that elderly runaway. Before I could ponder the matter at any length, a marvellous thing happened. I discovered the 'young adult' audience. My earlier novels had been well-received critically but had created no great stir although some readers dropped me a line. (No one ever telephoned.) Now suddenly I was beautifully besieged by my readers. They wrote letters. Telephoned. They listened in rapt attention when I spoke to them in classrooms or talked informally in cafeterias or on the steps outside. They questioned. They scolded. 'Why did you introduce Tubs Casper and get us interested in him and then drop him without another word – what happened to him, anyway?' I explained that Tubs Casper had been introduced as a device in order to depict a certain aspect of the situation. I was flattered that Tubs came alive for them, that they cared what happened to him. They pointed out, however, that I had let them down, that I had a responsibility to my readers, that I owed them the satisfaction of telling them *what had happened*. But life doesn't work out that way, I said. We don't find out everything about people in life, we aren't given all the answers, why should we expect all the answers in a novel that is exploring life as it is, not as it should be? There I was, discussing, debating, exploring aspects of fiction and the craft of writing with teenagers, and finding myself stimulated and enjoying myself immensely. While learning a thing or two about readers. And writing.

As indicated earlier, I did embark upon a sequel to *The Chocolate War*, motivated by the questions brought up by those young readers. They had made me curious: what *had* happened to Jerry Renault and Archie Costello and Brother Leon and all the others? What had the uneasy peace that had followed the chocolate war been like? Or had there been peace at all? (I don't always heavily plot my stories but often allow characters and events to sweep me along.) But I had misgivings. I remembered how much I had been disappointed by other sequels to books I'd enjoyed. Still, it was a challenge. But then a more compelling story idea came along, involving me emotionally as well as intellectually, and I put the sequel aside. The new book eventually became *I Am The Cheese*. As I surrendered myself to the agonies and delights of writing that novel, I realized that I was about to lose the young audience I had so recently discovered. Although the protagonist of *I Am The Cheese* is a teenage boy, the novel itself certainly wasn't being written with a teenage audience in mind. The construction was complex – three levels of storytelling operating almost simultaneously. Flashbacks within flashbacks. The story dealt with corruption in government – how interested could teenagers be in this topic? The good guys were not the winners – in fact, it was hard to tell the good guys from the bad guys. The plot was not neatly tied up with silk ribbons at the end. Indeed, the book did not really end at all in the conventional sense. I told myself: *say goodbye to the young adults* as I sent the manuscript off to my editor.

'The kids will love it,' he said when he called to tell me he wanted to publish the novel under the 'young adult' banner. 'It will make them angry and it will make them think. But they'll absorb it. They'll eat it up. Don't underestimate them,' he said.

His words were prophetic. *I Am The Cheese* seems to have found an even greater readership among young people than *The Chocolate War*. In fact, it sent new readers scurrying back to the earlier novel. *I Am The Cheese* was also read by adults. I received a letter from the mother of two teenagers who said she'd finally read the book after her daughter had practically browbeat her into it. She wrote: '*I Am The Cheese* is probably the first thing in years my daughter and I have agreed on – we loved it.' The paperback edition was released simultaneously as both an adult and YA novel.

The books have created some controversy along the way. Not everyone has agreed that *The Chocolate War* and *I Am The Cheese* are ideal reading fare for young people. Efforts were made in the small New England town of Groton, Massachusetts, to remove *The Chocolate War* from the high-school curriculum. A town hearing was held, conducted by the school committee. Impassioned speeches were made on both sides. Students signed petitions, in support of the novel. Parents were divided. Ultimately, the novel was retained in the curriculum and censorship was averted.

I Am The Cheese has also been troublesome to some people. A woman from Ohio recently wrote me a concerned letter, saying 'I would like to understand why you are writing young adult books with despair as the theme'. She accused me of turning young readers into 'absolute cynics at the age of twelve or less'. She signed the letter, 'Sincerely but with some anger'.

I don't doubt her sincerity or her concern or her anger, and I am still pondering how to answer her letter – I received it more than a month ago as I write this. My answer could be simple and glib and obvious. With violence rampant on the streets (often perpetrated, in fact, by young people) and corruption in high places reported daily in the newspapers and television broadcasts, is it possible to believe that my two books are turning youngsters into cynics? I could cite to her especially the dangers of television because it is not only the single biggest media influence on their lives but because of the way it sugarcoats its poison. Television feeds us violence and terror and assaults and yet manages to solve all these problems in time for the nine o'clock commercial. Television is telling our children from the moment they're able to follow plot and dialogue that the world is evil and the streets are unsafe but don't worry, Starsky and Hutch or Kojak are there to catch the bad guys before the station break. In the meantime, don't forget that the way to popularity is to protect from underarm odour. Perhaps, then, books like *The Chocolate War* or *I Am The Cheese* are antidotes to the sweet seductive poison of television.

I could present these arguments to that woman but I haven't as yet. Why? Because I have not quite accepted my role as a 'young adult' author and I have yet to write a 'young adult' novel. On the other hand, I know that my books are aimed by the publisher at young readers and I have accepted the rewards that have come from this development. I am also dismayed by being placed in the position of defending my novels. Shouldn't the novels speak for themselves?

Why should the author give explanations? The novels are written with truth to the situations and characters they portray with as much honesty as possible. Should more be asked of an author? In fact, should someone have to defend honesty and truth in his work?

Yet, I can appreciate that there are sensitive young people who could be upset by what happens in *The Chocolate War* and *I Am The Cheese*. As the father of three daughters and a son, I know the agonies that bringing up children in today's world presents. I also know that it's been impossible for me to protect them completely from the hazards and that I would be doing them a disservice by pretending to them that there is a guarantee of happiness on this planet of ours.

I know my own children, of course, but I have been learning about other children, children who call and write and ask questions in classrooms. And that perhaps brings us back to the questions posed earlier in this article. What to make of the telephone calls and letters I've received from young people? Perhaps the answer to that question is also the answer to that troubled woman who wrote in such anger and with such sincerity.

Take the letter written by the thirteen-year-old girl who said she had read *I Am The Cheese* twice. (Incidentally, she isn't alone in this – many others have said they've read it more than once to chase down the ambiguities.) In a world surrounded by the superficialities of our various media; the predigested books; the incessant sloganeering; the era of The Quick, from fast-foods to selfservice, this girl took the time to read a book twice and to write to the author. Or take the girl who said the book 'made me think'. With so many people ready to tell us what to do, what to wear, how to be happy, where to go, how to react, a teenager admits that a book made her think! That it happens to be my book thrills me beyond measure, that any book can do this in the face of today's mindlessness is cause to rejoice.

And the telephone call from that student in South Carolina. Have we the right to despair over the state of education and the purported disinterest of teachers and students when kids in a classroom are allowed by their teacher to call a writer a thousand miles away to settle a debate over a book? Doesn't this tell us something that has nothing to do with cynicism or despair although the book in question might have dealt with those elements?

Those ghostly phone calls asking for Amy Hertz are another

indication that a book is being read intently by young people, so intently and scrupulously that they take the trouble to actually dial a number in the book that might – just might – connect them with something in the novel. It is heartening to me that young readers can become involved in a novel to that extent.

Perhaps most heartening is what grew out of that attempt to ban *The Chocolate War* in that small New England town. After the controversy had died down and order was restored, the teacher who had been at the heart of the dispute invited me to visit her classroom. She said the students who had so ardently supported the novel wanted to meet the author. We had a grand time. Some of the students acted out scenes from the novel. We sat around informally discussing the book and the triumphant battle for its support. (It occurred to me that I have never received a protesting letter or comment from a youngster about the themes of my novels – only from adults.) Later, after the students had gone on to another class, the teacher said she wished to share an experience with me. She said it happened the day the class had decided to sponsor a petition on behalf of the novel, despite the opposition of some school committee members and even some of their parents. The word spread like wildfire because kids love to defy authority, parental or otherwise, of course. However, in the midst of the discussion about the petition, one student stood up to say: 'We should be unanimous about this. Everybody should sign it.' Another student leaped up: 'No,' he said. 'That's the kind of thing that happened in *The Chocolate War*. If anybody doesn't want to sign the petition, they shouldn't have to.'

The teacher said: 'That was worth the controversy, the headaches, all of it. They'd really learned something from it all. It made my day.'

It also made mine.

9 Muir's manure: the role of the critic

Robert Leeson

In the horticulture of children's books, critics are the fertilizer. So said Frank Muir when he opened the 'Children's Books of the Year' exhibition in 1978. It was a piece of impudence which obliged all critics present to laugh louder than anyone else. But the obvious insult which reflects a popular attitude towards the general run of criticism, obscured a little the other aspect of his image, by which he intended to show what role the critic/reviewer might play in the world of books for young people.

I thought again about this remark in mid-winter as I spent a weekend spreading half a ton of horse manure over the allotment. It was a laborious process, the benefits of which I could not expect to see immediately. Indeed they would only show themselves when what had been spread had disintegrated and dispersed throughout the soil.

I'm not sure if many reviewers liked Muir's version of their role any better than they liked his more obvious reference to their un-popularity. Critics, no less human than writers, editors, teachers, librarians and parents, like their part in affairs to be more immediately recognizable and acceptable. Perhaps they prefer to be seen as the arranger of beautiful flowers in cut glass, or the exhibitor of rare plants carefully cultivated, or (more satisfying) the dispenser of instant death through a verbal aerosol to one of the more obnoxious weeds.

But manure? That's another matter. To use your position as reviewer, slowly to permeate the world of books for young people, seeking to enrich, to boost crop yield, to contribute to abundance. That's a social, promotional role that would not suit everyone. Yet it seems to me that in the long run Muir is right and the best part a reviewer can play in this particular field of reading, is a fertilizing one.

Or to put it another way. The real task for the reviewer is not to erect fresh landmarks in children's literature, but rather to change the landscape.

And, since we are talking about a literary landscape which over the past two centuries has become more and more cultivated, then manure it must be.

This may appear to involve a loss of independence for the critic. But, then, I would reject the notion of such 'independence' for critic or for writer, from the rest of the people who are involved with young people and books, to the extent that this implies isolation or detachment. Objectivity should not imply disengagement. For we are engaged in a period of far reaching change, engaged in the sense that though much of the change is happening whether we like it or not, yet we are also active within it, encouraging or resisting.

There is an extreme critical point of view which, faced with the controversy over the nature and meaning of children's literature, asserts that the whole business is best left between 'the ivory tower and the market place'. This is not intended to mean that the writer should be left to the mercy of market forces (though that happens often enough) but that the tug of war which goes on between creativity and commerce is preferable to any direct and conscious public influence and involvement.

There is in this point of view a certain illusion – that the market place is simply a mechanical contrivance and that it has no subjective, no ideological element. In fact we know that there's ideology in the market place and in the ivory tower too. One thing we can see in the current argument over critical criteria in children's books is the belated recognition by a number of the parties involved, that like the old person who found she'd been talking in quotations all her life, they have been politicians all along without knowing it.

Any hope of a pure detachment in the business of criticism is a dying one. We may strive to keep heads level, to retain our objectivity and independent frame of mind, examining ourselves for signs of prejudice, opinions of convenience, second-hand ideas and so forth, but we are engaged, like it or not, and it's a matter of the best use of our abilities, given that recognition.

In any case, as we know, the 'market place' has lamentably failed the younger generation. It has not found it 'worthwhile' to place bookshops in most of the areas where our young people live. Without some kind of deliberate and conscious public intervention through area library, school library, school and community bookshop, the majority of youngsters would still not be able to make *any* choice between ivory tower and market place. And even in areas where the public has ready access to the book through commercial channels, the normal rules do not apply. The purchaser is not generally the consumer. Most books read by young people, even teenagers, come to them through the intervention of a second party.

Ironically it is the social action, and in many cases voluntary labour of teachers and others through the school bookshops (the best thing since wholemeal bread) which has restored (or initiated) some kind of personal 'commercial' choice in pupils' reading matter.

We critics do not offer our wit and wisdom to a world of free floating individuals, making isolated individual choices from an instantly and universally available range of books. If that 'world' ever existed for adults, it certainly does not for young readers.

So I think the first criterion for a reviewer must be a realization at some level or other of the nature of the consumer, the way in which he or she comes to books and the world in which the books are read. This brings us up against another argument – book-centred criticism versus reader or child-centred criticism. It may be thought that one can preserve a genuine independence by fixing one's mind on the book and not flickering one eye at the 'market'. But is this really the case?

Is it not possible that those who try consciously to eliminate the image of the potential young reader from the mind, are instead allowing another 'spiritual' child to guide the mental process. Not your rough-cut, multi-coloured, Grange Hill child, but your pink well-bred, well-housed and certainly well-read child of yesteryear?

As some writers say they write for 'the child they once were', so may some critics. It has an attractive and 'natural' ring but it was always a partial view. And today, the children we once were live in a very different world.

And again, which child? If we accept that we keep in mind the child who might read the book, while still keeping an eye on the book itself, and if we accept that today's young reader looks, talks and acts somewhat differently, is that enough? I don't think so. Today we must consider not only the young reader, but the non-reader. Or rather, bearing in mind the millions who read comics and magazines, some of considerable technical complexity, the young non-book reader or the young non-regular book reader. And that is to say, the majority.

Yet this does not mean taking each book in turn and saying – this will do for the keen reader but it won't bring in any new members to the club, so it's no good. It's a matter of saying that if you come across a book which can appeal to both keen reader and unwilling reader then you welcome it even more.

It's a general rule that the book which will appeal to the unwilling reader will also appeal to the willing. To that extent the willing are privileged, they get two meals to the unwilling's one. Some people will say that far too much attention is paid to the unwilling readers who have, believe it or not, no less than eighty series of books devoted to attracting them (between the ages of seven and seventeen). But if one says that one is looking above all for books for the willing, which will also reach out to the unwilling, then the converse ought to apply – that books for the unwilling must also reach out towards the willing.

The willing reader is generally omnivorous, not to say gluttonous and will read anything, from the back of the cornflake packet to the captions on their mate's magazine on the bus, and will even, while holding their own reading matter, try and read someone else's as well.

Yet if reading matter for the unwilling left lying around will not even make the willing bat an eyelid, then it is too poor for the unwilling.

I have always felt that critics who disregard special series for the unwilling reader are neglecting their duty. If the critic's job is to choose, then prejudice must not do a preselection job. But little better is the attitude which says – these books are OK for the un-willing reader but for no one else. This is a kind of critical attention which helps to carry deprivation to a new more modern level. We critics owe more generous critical attention to reading for the un-willing reader, not as a thing in itself, all right for those who have to have that sort of thing. Reading for the unwilling must, I think, be judged as a contribution to creating a kind of literature which will have universal appeal, to the widest range of young reader.

To put it in a matter of fact way. At the end of a year in which I as an editor and critic have to oversee the reviewing, selecting and rejecting of something like 800–1,000 books for young people of all ages, what conclusion am I to draw? Have we selected a dozen pearls which will still be 'classics' when our children have children, or have we chosen a range of say 80 to 100 books from which parent-teacher-librarian may choose to lay before the potential reader/buyer.

This larger number may or may not contain gems. But I take leave to doubt that we should spend our critical lives like fanatical prospectors exploding mountains into debris for the sake of the solitary gleam.

In my travels around the country I often ask teachers and librarians how much notice they take of reviews in the press. Very rarely will they admit to taking any. This may be professional pride and the wish to appear independent. Perhaps, after all, most critical work can only build or undermine writers' reputations over a period, seeping gradually into the consciousness of the middle men and women who see that the books reach the young people.

But, on the other hand, the most active librarians and teachers do get together to review books before and after publication. As a writer I find the most fascinating reviews of my own books are those prepared for strictly internal use.

Now there is a certain condescension at the top towards the standard of professional choice among librarians and teachers. Yet even this tune is changing. When it first appeared the unofficial teacher-written Review Sheet in London was regarded in 'the trade' with mingled rage and contempt as its cutting edge reached those parts of literary reputations other critics could not reach. Today it's a different matter. Such 'little' papers have become a kind of *samizdat* in top children's literary circles.

But this kind of reviewing comes from rank and file teachers and librarians at their most active and informed. There are many thousands who are just not aware of the range of books which exist. Some indeed, are not even aware that they are not aware. They know of excellent tried and trusted books, written perhaps twenty years ago, and see no need to venture further. But those who are aware of their unawareness do not generally feel that our work as critics helps them much. For them a carefully annotated selection of recent books is worth more than a measured study of the latest Garfield or Garner.

Such selections may not be regarded as show pieces of criticism, but to do them well, one needs to know a lot, to think carefully and exercise one's judgment *invisibly* and without the flourish which earns the smile from a casual journal reader. It's back to the manure business. Whatever my own readers think of my standards of criticism, this is the form in which they most actively request it from me. It is a sobering thought.

Now a critique which bears in mind the child, the parent, teacher, librarian, also tends in the long run to be labelled as being of the didactic school, more concerned with the *use* of the book than its intrinsic quality. Superficial as this label is, it is not simply to be dismissed.

The dispute over meaning and message, over bias in the literature for young people has recently, I'm happy to say, come out into the open, although this means it has become more strident and prone to misrepresentation. Parties have formed, Aesthetes versus Didacts (like Cavaliers and Roundheads) which have ridden round the land tearing down each other's proclamations and rallying the well-affected to their side. Whole communities of book-handlers have been subjected to hose-pipe conversion.

Some would have it that those who seek to introduce open and public criteria for the judgment of books for young people, for example, raising the question of race, class or sex bias, are a new and alien intrusion into the traditional, dignified 'natural' way of choosing a *good* book. Some would argue, on the contrary, that it is simply a new outbreak of Puritanism or Trimmerism, which plagues the literature every now and then.

I would say that what is happening is both new and old, and what is old in it is very old indeed. It is the distinguished and honourable argument over the relation of form to content, art to nature, which has gone on since Aristotle was a lad and probably before. Over a couple of thousands of years there have been waves of change in both form and content, though content changes more often than form, which tends to be the conservative element. Both are legitimate subjects for debate and always have been. If content were not to be debated and changed, then most written tales would still be about kings and queens, gods and goddesses. If form were eternal, then the epic and lay would never have given way to the novel, short story, poem and play.

When a literature establishes itself, as children's has over the past two centuries, it tends by the accumulated practice of its craftsfolk (helped or hindered by their critics) to develop a high level of expertise, and to become more and more obsessed with form. This is so in all branches – medieval geste, Restoration drama, classic novel. Nothing was more rigid and repetitive, yet expert in its way, than the prewar children's novel, historical, school or domestic.

Postwar changes in content owe a good deal to outside pressures to the development of a new readership, a new market, new social scene. No amount of purely 'aesthetic' judgment could have displaced that old reading matter. Critics could only have gone on arguing about how well or how badly the old ideas were portrayed. The postwar development and turmoil in young people's literature exists partly because within the circle of writers, critics and their fellows, the body of literary experience was just not large enough to match the social body of experience seeking expression. Hence the apparent intrusion into the ivory tower. It's a necessary shake-up, uncomfortable for some writers and critics, but in the end bound to do good.

But, when the dust has settled (not for a while yet I believe) reviewers will not sit down and count mechanically the number of women, blacks or workers in the average book and estimate their status according to some new statutory yardstick. On the contrary, it will be our aesthetic senses which will have been expanded in the sense that we shall be aware that writing which treats certain people as though they are invisible, or condescends to them or misrepresents them, is lacking not simply socially, but in failing to represent rounded characters in a true situation. Our developing mental equipment as critics will include a greater awareness of a changing world and its effect upon a changing body of young people, whether they are habitual readers or not.

For young people in their teens this is a far more disorientating time than we adults can possibly realize. There is the old, the classic problem of growth. Children before puberty are aware every now and then that they have changed. There are things they once could not do and now can. But the present, the acceptance of change is all. From puberty on, for a few very concentrated years, the change itself is the dominant element in their lives. Physical restlessness of an often unbearable kind goes along with feelings of instability in all relations with one and other and with the adult world.

For the first time they actively realize that they are separate from their parents and other adults and yet must inevitably become like them, or of that kind.

For some at this stage, books are a valuable source of reassurance, a source of information about life which seems independent of the real adults they know. Stories can offer explanations of behaviour by contemporaries or older people which are credible in their fullness where mini-lectures or even sympathetic conversations are not. The writer who can successfully reach the teenage child has the happy status of favoured aunt, uncle or older friend whose views may be listened to, accepted or rejected without comeback or consequence.

This factor influences many books for 'new adults' which seek to tide the reader over from the rejection of 'children's books' (if the teenager ever read a children's book) to the limitless variety of the adult book. Unfortunately all too many of these 'new adult' books which I have seen as a critic have a weakness which must limit their appeal. I do not refer to the didactic element in them as such, but to the nature of the advice offered. All too often the theme is 'coming to terms' (now almost a dirty phrase in the critical vocabulary – indeed a critic once praised a book of mine as being one in which 'nobody comes to terms with anything'). The main purpose behind this phrase 'coming to terms' seems to be that the teenage reader should understand that his or her view of the world is immature, will change, and that what they now reject, they will accept. In many ways this is true, but the underlying assumption is that the young person is in the wrong, which may not be the case. Their instincts, if not their judgment, or their tactics, may be sound, even if their ability to re-order their world is strictly limited.

The number of such books which genuinely sympathise with the teenager *from the inside* is very limited, though on the increase. It is, above all, a matter of refining the critic's or chooser's rapport with the reader, meeting their needs at a disturbing time of life.

If it is difficult to judge the younger child of today by means of the child 'one once was', it is infinitely more so to judge the teenager, who is changing rapidly in a rapidly changing world, when the credibility of the older generation as managers of life is constantly undermined by the evidence of the young person's eyes.

I would wish all writers to meet the young people they are considered to write for. Through the schools this is fortunately easier than it was. I would also wish the critics to meet and talk with 3f and 4b, and not simply to talk but to listen. Or to sit unobtrusively, as I've done on more than one occasion, during a lunch hour in a bookshop at a big secondary school, to watch the customers come and go and see the choices they make and the discussions they have with the shopkeeper. They are often looking for a book (in the abstract) which is not there. Yet it may well exist, or something very like it. To bring book and reader or potential reader together is an immensely important and satisfying achievement.

We have on the one hand an immense potential readership and on the other a rich and developing literature. They need to be brought together more and the literature helped to grow to meet that readership's needs. This is the most impressive task that criticism can set itself. It's a wide ranging and at the same time an unobtrusive aim. It is working for less than immediate gain, to be achieved when the impelling counsel or words and their source may well be forgotten, but none the less worthwhile for that.

10 Lighting the blue touch paper: the importance of television

Peter Plummer

Never again so generous, never again so jealous; never so angry, never so much in love; never so hurt, never so hurtful. Here, blood-stained and bloodyminded, the teenager comes stumbling through the marble palace with the terrifying abruptness of an Orestes or a Medea. Such a concentration of emotion is a heady and potent rocket fuel, whether for author or television director (and a basic reason for my own eternal fascination with the years that begin the moment that Kim sits in the bazaar and starts to question the nature of identity). It is as if in our teens we are – in some form – everything we shall ever be – but never again to a degree so intense. Years of a violent myth which we learn, with age, to ritualise into socially acceptable performances.

But to handle the raw material in the pre-ritual stage, the stage when the explorations are still being made and the finger-tips rubbed sore at every hand-hold on the cliff-face – this I have always felt to be one of the most privileged and exciting opportunities offered by television drama. If these very unstructured thoughts are anything then they are an attempt to come to terms with the teachers and publishers who are always demanding to know why it was *that* particular book that got to the television screen and why it was done in *that* particular way and what, really, *are* the considerations that circumscribe the relationship of teenage fiction to its television adaptation. And hereinafter I'm allowing myself the indulgence of reference to fiction written for teenagers as TF and adaptations thereof for television as TFA – not least because the small 't' on my typewriter is somewhat recalcitrant – though it does at least allow the unobstructed operation of the even more crucial key above it.

£££££££££££££

Newtons. And to those who have to budget whether for books or television, alarmingly less responsive to gravity than the old tons.

But it is money that ultimately affects decisions in television quite as much as in publishing (and the wage-cost spiral has had quite as much effect on the one as the other in the service industries). When OUP published *Flambards* in hardback in 1967 (the usual superlative Oxford binding and polythened dust-jacket) it retailed at 17s 6d! *Edge of the Cloud* and *Flambards in Summer* followed in 1969 at 18s apiece.

At exactly the same period, *The Owl Service* television location crew stayed overnight at their hotel for less than two hundred pounds all in. Today, twice that amount would come nowhere near getting a crew into an equivalent hotel.

And all this was particularly important for TFA. As (largely) novels of movement, space and location (and young people's correspond-ence to us reveals very clearly the remarkable power which a visually unusual and haunting location can exercise upon them) they are usually the *least* suited to being brought back to the confines of the studio (yes, there *have* been honourable exceptions!) And all the time, the cinema was an important touchstone as a potent reminder of the effects Big Money could achieve.

From the moment in the early fifties when the BBC bought up the RKO film library (and, subsequently, in the mid-fifties when Lew Grade secured the UAA Warner Brothers library for ITV) British television, whether it liked it or not, was inviting direct comparison in the living room between the production values of the superbudget commercial film and the run-of-the-mill television drama with which it stood shoulder-to-shoulder in the transmission schedules. Not that what costs most is best, but anything that *looks* cheap is always a shoddy embarrassment.

And so, inevitably, there has been a change in the kind of material which television has sought to appropriate to itself. Today, for example, I'm sure that most of us would feel that Granada's adapta-tions of the Capt. W. E. Johns' *Biggles* stories, produced for television nearly twenty years ago, would look pretty untransmittable. Shot in what would now seem a very small studio with cramped facilities it gave rise on one occasion to the memorable designer's quote: 'Well, we might squeeze a *quarter* of a Messerschmitt into here pro-vided you could play the rest of the show in a telephone kiosk – but if you want to leave room for the cameras of course, you'll have to do without the kiosk.'

Today, one of our massive drama studios could probably absorb half a squadron of Messerschmitts – if we didn't opt for location filming anyway. But the costs of the latter don't just lie in hotels. Time is money. It's been said of location drama units that they're always waiting around for one of two things – the sun to go in or the sun to come out (I well remember having to shoot the torrential rainstorm at the end of *The Owl Service* in the hottest, most cloudless June that our Welsh valley had ever known).

And if going on location costs money, then going into *period*, whether on location or in the studio, costs even more. And the ultimate nightmare for a programme committee session (one for which the lacing of mid-morning coffee with valium should be mandatory) is any suggestion of going on location, in period, in a foreign setting.

But most of today's television companies, their producers, their directors and their designers have learned by bitter experience that if a thing's worth doing, then it's worth doing at the right price or not at all. And 'not at all' can often be the right decision. But

One there was that had a project for a tower of jade –
Three matchstick boxes were his present stock in trade.

Such a projector must have been whoever assumed that Prince Edward Island could be adequately conjured up in a BBC studio (and not a big one by the look of it) for *Anne of Avonlea*. By contrast, the BBC's *The Mill on the Floss*, with just enough of a location budget to allow the obsessively litigated Dorlcote Mill its due prominence, was a visual pleasure.

But the altogether new financial dimension of the past decade has, of course, been the international co-production. In essence, this is a deal whereby two or more production funders in different countries (not all of whom themselves actually need have studio capacity) agree jointly to finance a project, usually in return for the exclusive rights of distribution within their own territories. Britain's current reputation as the world's leader in standards of television production has enabled it to carve a major share in such deals (including a major share also in the actual production work).

There is an enormously fruitful future here for drama adaptations for younger viewers – and in some possibly surprising directions. I emphasize the latter because so many people seem to assume that language has bound us forever to a transatlantic tethering post. Not so.

Europe has been dubbing Hollywood's commercial output now for so long, that language problems have paled. No question either (as anyone will know who has ever been with a widely representative international gathering of teenagers) that in everything except language, young Europeans seem to have a surprisingly greater affinity with each other, than with their transatlantic counterparts. Styles of education, emphases of curriculum, attitudes of family, forms of sport and the roles of the state in their lives – all have vastly more in common with each other in Western Europe than with the American pattern. It's hardly surprising that English parents who have had both American and European youngsters in the home as guests should find that the American is a charming, but somehow 'entirely different' sort of animal – vastly more mature in some respects, vastly less so in others.

It's true that the States is the only nation in which TF is organized as a major industry, but that industry has nevertheless had signally little joy (so far) in pushing its enormous publishing successes out of the library and bookshop into television (though signs are that a big lobby is currently being coordinated and, as President Roosevelt said, the Big American Lobby is just a longer way of writing 'inevitability'). For the present, however, as an American teacher once said to me, 'American television for the over-sevens is frankly crap, because as far as American television is concerned there are *no* American children over the age of seven. They're all goddam eight or nine-year-olds going on twenty.'

A pity, because it would be nice to see some sympathetic adaptations of Hinton or Zindel. Above all, an uninflated treatment of Monte Linkletter's magnificent great original, *Cricket Smith*, would surely be a joy. Both the comic set-pieces and the ultimate anguish of the latter seem to me to be informed with an almost un-American objectivity – to the point of being superb international viewing. But if it ever reaches any screen, then I guess it would probably be the big one. My hunch is that the only transatlantic hopes for TFA lie worlds away from either of our cultures – among the fantasy writers.

I have to concede that we in television perhaps haven't always done as much homework as we might into the very considerable overseas successes of some of our own writers – and in particular, the special localized success of certain writers in certain countries (indeed, in our own country, do we pick up the hints offered in any bookseller's magazine – like the fact that Hardy's comet is still rising while George Bernard Shaw is currently a dusty back number). But I've often supposed that the BBC were more aware than some of the present vast international translation market in Thomas Hardy – not least in unexpected places like Japan. The fact that Japan is also acquainted with some of our English young people's fiction prompts me to suggest that publishers might occasionally like to back their adaptation suggestions with details of their own overseas publication successes.

At least one recent co-production had surely been preceded by homework and market investigation. Some years ago, the German firm of Boje Verlag negotiated to publish in hardback and paperback a small selection of the work of Leon Garfield – including *Jack Holborn* and *Black Jack*. The venture was highly successful and, as a result, the same firm then contracted for the German rights to *Prisoners of September*, *Mister Corbett's Ghost* and *The Ghost Downstairs*. This meant that both Britain and Germany shared a 'prepared market' for Garfield. Not in the sense that he was a household name in either country (how many writers are, even in the world of adult fiction?) but insofar as television executives in both countries knew that among their younger viewers, as well as in libraries and bookshops, there was a rising currency in Garfield's coin. (It was fascinating to learn [*School Bookshop News*, No. 11, Autumn 1978] that Garfield has been pursuing the German connection in the plot of his latest book.) This was the sound basis for the setting up of a co-production deal between Hessische Rundfunk and the BBC in respect of Garfield's superb *Strange Affair of Adelaide Harris*. The result has been a splendid production with a glorious cast and some attractive ideas in the sets (the inn, it is true, was perhaps excessively timid, but the Foundlings Home was a joy). Sad only that its transmission time meant that most adults were deprived of a view of the perplexed balloon-face of Freddie Jones' baffled Raven.

Sadly, many of the criteria which make a book a non-runner for TFA co-production will, of course, also rule it out in respect of any company wanting to go it alone. We still have a legacy of taboos (one of the main reasons why I suspect *Cricket Smith* will get on to the cinema screen before it reaches our living rooms). Any classroom of children will tell you very precisely and in identical terms (whatever their social background) the order of antipathies as far as the British parent is concerned:

Bad language is taboo number one.
Sex comes second.
Violence a poor third.

Almost *never*, in my experience, has a viewer ever complained about the basic morality of a drama presentation (e.g. the idea that the acquisition of wealth is to be equated with 'making good').

Parents do, however, seem to bring some extraordinary fantasies to their viewing. I well remember one angry father who complained (following an episode of *The Intruder* in which Jane and Arnold had been sun-bathing on the sea-church island) that he had witnessed a rape (a pure figment of his imagination of course). His final argument was that no girls ought to be seen in bathing-costumes in young people's drama because the assumption must be that they had either just taken part in or were about to take part in sexual intercourse.

There is no question, however, that in respect of bad language, sex or violence, the author has a much easier 'get-out' than the poor television director. Quite inoffensive for the author to write 'he swore', but how, while remaining inoffensive, does the actor portray that swearing?

At the climax of *The Intruder*, the central Arnold–Jane relationship turns on just such a point. Is such a magnificent book to be rejected for adaptation on this count? If not, then is the passage in question to be omitted? But this is to omit Townsend's absolutely crucial distinction of values. The hero, Arnold, smashing a way to safety for himself and Jane inside a flooded church literally 'swears his way through a brick wall'.

He swore between blows, swore at the top of his voice, swore and hit, swore and hit.

They reach safety. Jane clings to him for warmth, excited by him, his action, his achievement. The memory of the swearing makes her giggle. But later, at a distance in time and place, the boy who saved her life assumes a new image in her mind.

She shuddered, recalling the crude repetition, the crude accent. That had been dreadful, part of the nightmare. She could hardly believe she had giggled afterwards, had clung to Arnold. That couldn't have been her. That was somebody else, a character in the film that kept projecting itself in the corners of her mind.

We had already had problems over 'bad' language in *The Owl Service*. Alan Garner had felt strongly that Gwyn's sense of utter betrayal by Alison and her mother and by his own mother, demanded something approximating to a vomit of words to match the image of his tiny figure struggling away over the mountain top. Accordingly, he scripted Gwyn to turn a pack (nay, a maul) of rugby songs into a torrent of wind-blown abuse at those he has left behind him below in the valley. Violent parental objections ensued – mostly, curiously enough, from rugby-playing fathers who felt that such things were 'designed only for the changing room and the bar'. I should add that Alan undertook to write to them all personally himself!

But when we came to *The Intruder* we could hardly say we hadn't been warned. In the end we permitted Arnold a few milder (and IBA-agreed) oaths before allowing the sound of storm and flood to drown his voice. But in terms of John Rowe Townsend's intention it was, I'm afraid, a cop-out. Happily, he understood our predicament.

It's important to add, however, that within quite short periods public attitudes can undergo a considerable change. Both *The Intruder* and *The Owl Service* were repeated some years after their original transmission. Have certain authors now acquired an unquestioned respectability? I only know that on a second showing neither programme provoked a single viewer's protest!

The considerable difficulties associated with screen violence, however, led us two or three years ago into a decision which had curious results. Granada commissioned a further serial from Alan Garner. When it duly appeared it was *Red Shift* and an obvious problem. There was no way in which it would have been fair to viewers to transmit it (as *The Owl Service* and *The Intruder* had been transmitted) at Sunday tea-time. The traditions of this particular and hallowed TFA 'time-slot' I'll discuss in a moment, but at the time in question the result of our quandary was that we had to write off our

option money and let Garner's serial fall by the wayside. Subsequently, of course, *Red Shift* appeared as a hardback novel – with the
bookshops obviously at a loss to know in which department to
shelve it! At the BBC they chose to see it as an entirely adult property
which they duly acquired – so what had started off as a Granada
young people's drama commission finished up on the BBC as a very
adult-angled 9.25 p.m. *Play for Today*!

There has recently been a revolution in attitudes to TFA transmission time and it's worth examining for a moment something of
the history of custom and practice in this respect. Whether on BBC
or ITV there is a very natural and understandable tendency for peak
programme budgetting to become synchronous with peak viewing
times. There is, after all, no point in spending a fortune on a
Christmas Spectacular if you then transmit it at 3 a.m. on Boxing
Day morning. Now, far back in broadcasting history, BBC radio
Children's Hour (of blessed memory) established what might almost
be described as a media metabolism for childhood. It determined
with a typically Reithian precision the hour (5 p.m. to 6 p.m.) at
which the junior population of the British Isles should be granted
their allowance of the ether. It was never a programme for babes
in arms, for those who, having heard it, could expect to be dispatched
immediately to bed. In fact, by any standards of pure consideration
for its child listeners it was in many ways a rather *un*suitable hour of
transmission. Except in those houses where tea was served twice,
tea-time tended to be when Dad came home. And Dad came home
rather later in the thirties and forties than he does now. For the
younger ones, playtime with one's mates was that blessed after-
school period before tea-time. For the older ones, with homework,
the pre-tea-time period was the best chance to get the stuff done
before small brothers and sisters came in from play and before Dad
came home. Bang into the middle of these precious moments came
the equally precious (for it was) *Children's Hour* with its potent
demand for attention. And so childhood's day, as Henry Hall's band
happily reiterated, had a precisely prescribed end:

> At six o'clock their mummies and daddies
> Will take them home to bed
> Because they're tired little teddy bears.

Naturally, their mummies and daddies did nothing of the sort ,but that was the myth. In fact, of course, every child appeared at school the next morning with all the latest gags from last night's ITMA. Equally, it has been known almost since the inception of television, that children's viewing enjoyment and list of 'favourite programmes' is by no means confined to those shown during the accepted tea-time children's slot. Indeed, the transition to an active enjoyment of 'adult' programmes seems to be well under way as early as the ages of eight to eleven, while among older children the preference for adult television drama is overwhelming.

Favourite Kinds of Programmes

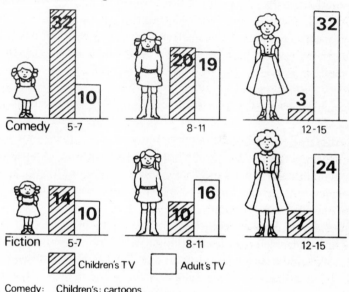

Comedy 5-7   8-11   12-15

Fiction 5-7   8-11   12-15

Children's TV   Adult's TV

Comedy:	Children's:	cartoons
	Adults':	comedy & light entertainment
Fiction:	Children's:	drama
	Adults':	films, plays, adventure/action, romance

The table printed above derives from researches initiated by the IBA in conjunction with the ITV Network Children's Sub-committee some four or five years ago (see 'Children and Television' by Dr Mallory Wober in *Independent Broadcasting*, No. 2, November 1974). It needs to be said, and the researchers themselves have clearly said it, that all such observations should be as stuffed with qualifications as a fellow of All Souls, but none the less it seems pretty clear that by the age of eleven, and probably a good deal before that, children's main television drama viewing lies well out of *'Children's Hour'*. As between the child and the adult, the teenager tends, of course, in television schedules as in life, to be in no-man's land. *Top of the Pops* has remained television's only regular evening nod in the direction of teenage drama (which is what, in a sense, it is). Any more orthodox drama material for this age group has tended to get funnelled by both channels, for lack of any better inspiration, into a Sunday tea-time half-hour where it must take turn and turn about over the months with material designed for rather younger viewers. Purely as a transmission time it is not without its considerable merits but it does, sadly, carry with it the associations of *Children's Hour*:

> My mate happened to see it and he told me about it. I don't bother to watch then because it's usually kids things that time of day . . .

Such was the way one adolescent came to start watching *The Intruder*.

Above all (or rather, below most) it is not a slot that can regularly be expected to carry the production budget weighting of a peak time show. Which brings us to Mrs Peyton's *Flambards* trilogy.

Television people interested in TFA have been trying to hook their programme committees on Mrs Peyton's trilogy ever since *Flambards in Summer* reached the bookshelves back in 1969. Stella Richman brooded over it for London Weekend Television, trying to find a way of securing an 'adult' budget for it. I myself finished reading it on holiday in the Mediterranean, wrote to Mrs Peyton and sent what I hoped was a sufficiently passionate cable to Granada urging the purchase of an option (I even got up some hopeful tests on radio-controlled model aircraft on my return). But everybody everywhere foundered on the budget. When Mrs Peyton said recently:

> The filming of *Flambards* has been going to happen for the last ten years, ever since it was first written, but I had become innured to disappointment as plans inevitably fell through . . .

I knew exactly what she felt like, but it was simply not worth doing if the hunt was going to have to consist of half a dozen rocking horses. Nor is it a matter of a single company finding enough money – in ITV it's also a matter of what share of the network pay-back kitty is available. And peak viewing times command the peak money.

When *Flambards* finally reached the television screen, under the patronage of Yorkshire Television, it did so because, in a major break with tradition, the network contractors agreed to accept a television adaptation of a book from the children's shelves in peak viewing time. And not by halves either – the first episode ran for ninety minutes! It just could be that the implications of the ITV Network children's sub-committee research project have at last been accepted, namely, that TFA could make at least as good peak-hour family viewing as much of whatever else passes under that label.

Whether Leonard Lewis' production of *Flambards* for Yorkshire Television has been an auspicious innovation in this respect is, sadly, a different matter. *Anybody* who can contrive, by whatever means, to get hold of a literary property that excites them and then raise a budget to get it shot and on to the screen has achieved one hell of a lot. It's about a thousand times more difficult than getting a book published, I would suppose. Hats off, then, for this. And hats off too for the best things in that version of *Flambards*. The superb visuals of the Bramham Moor hunt in the first episode; the magnificent work throughout of David Boddington on the flying sequences (three full-scale planes were constructed, designed to taxi but not to fly, the latter being done by splendidly organized and filmed remote-control models); and Sebastian Abineri's perfectly self-contained yet entirely individualized performance as Dick.

But one feels that so much more, so very much more (not least the whole future of evening TFA) depended on this production being as nearly as possible an unqualified success. And the qualifications (oh please don't think this is wine squeezed from sour grapes – it's my very heart's blood) are, alas, too many.

With one outstanding exception (the self-indulgent music compounded with an extraordinary decision to bring it 'forward' in the sound mix) they are the pitfalls of all TFA (and, heaven knows, I've been covered in mud myself a good few times in the past). So they may at least serve as a kind of writers' and publishers' guide to the specific minefields that TF adaptation and production involve.

Despite Mrs Peyton's own unquestioned optimism on first meet-ing the cast (and what a daunting hall of mirrors that can be for any writer!) the event has sadly proven that perfect looks alone simply cannot carry a central character. Will's adrenalin is the fuel of the first two books of the trilogy. Christina is pulled into his slipstream almost in spite of herself. His hand is on the joy-stick and the rev count comes from him. But tragically, this Will did not find a way and, perhaps because of under-rehearsal, I can't feel that he really achieved take-off speed. In a young and comparatively inexperienced cast it became all too easy for the others to slump to his tempo. And I've been responsible for *exactly* the same disasters myself in the past and watched young actors near the end of the day falling disastrously into step, beat for beat, and I've looked at the clock and remembered the schedule and known that time was running out and wished, oh if you poor young things had only that extra year of technique to save us from a retake and this is another fine mess I've gotten us into . . .

Just about every one of us in this business must, at some time or other, have suffered the same disaster in casting an adolescent role. It's a leap into the darkest of darks. Looks, charm, personality, intelligence, sensitivity – all these may be there. A screen test goes beautifully. But ahead lie anything up to thirteen consecutive hours of drama, the production work of perhaps an entire year. Will the stamina be there? Will the concentration hold? Or will it all fall apart after a month or so and will the director find that everyone else is having to be neglected at rehearsal because a permanent prop is needed for a very tender shoot?

It's impossible to overemphasize the importance of this. TFA will always be essentially about T. In no other form of drama are T consistently such central features. Yes, of course we can see them serving as camera fodder in family situation comedies for the sake of their so-funny gaucheries and in police drama as archetypal mindless hoodlums, but vastly more demanding on the young actor is the sustained observation of a serialization that turns either comic or hoodlum archetype into an individual.

The writer has it so easy! Take, as perhaps extreme examples, two intense expressions of cerebral energy – the grail quests of the boy in John Rowe Townsend's *Forest of the Night* and of Donald in William Mayne's *A Game of Dark*. The behaviour of both characters is circumscribed solely by the limits of the writer's vision. On television, for all the tricks, illusions and technical mayhem of which the screen is capable, a new limit is imposed on the original. The script type-face is now meaningless until you find an adolescent actor with the sensitivity to receive and the technique to re-transmit the compulsive and driving urgency of those same pilgrimages.

For TFA's insights must surely relate to the individual rather than to the gang. TF is about identity. It's about leaving the age of the Secret Sixes, Famous Fives and Filthy Fours behind you. It starts, as I said before, with the question that Kim asks himself in the teeming bazaar – who am I and what am I? And yes, the experimental apparatus for discovering identity is relationship. But that's a world away from the gang and the gang book, where the allocations of dialogue to individuals are often pretty well interchangeable a lot of the time. Much easier to cast and direct though. At least, according to Robert Mulligan describing his experiences in handling a group of American teenage actors in his film *Summer of 42*:

> Oddly enough, with teenagers, because they're bright and intelligent – and they go to the movies and maybe they've acted in high school – all you have to do is show them how to behave, to do what comes naturally. You have to calm them down so that they listen to one another.

Yes, but then pull them out of Phi Beta Kappa and put them on their lonesome ownsome facing the hot stench of Worm or Tyger. Gangland is child's play.

No question either that it's generally easier for the talented actor in his mid teens to put on a false beard and spout Polonius than to stand on stage and produce any sort of statement within a pure teenage persona. Where can you hide *you*?

And the more desirable the material, of course, the greater the difficulty in materializing it. On the available evidence (and please send me details of any review that refutes this) I would be led to suppose that an adequate stage, film or television presentation of Shakespeare's *Romeo and Juliet* was unachievable. Lines delivered at face-value seem to be all that we can hope for. And so, we get seduced into supposing that this monstrous pair were sweet blameless lovers instead of arrogant, hypersensitive show-offs, desperately hyping up experience like shots of a mind-blowing drug. But what twentieth century fifteen-year-olds have the capacity to recognize (let alone put across) the gross self-indulgence which inflates every line of their verse and makes the plot no footling 'accidental' tragedy but one deriving essentially and inevitably from the characters of the young lovers and their massive vanity. The dread opposition of surnames, of course, simply made for more hype, more kicks, and if ever a play had a villain then surely Friar John was the Dr Timothy Leary of his age. Charlie Manson's girls could tell you a thing or two about Shakespeare's Mantua. So could Patty Hearst. After the event.

But there's the problem. Casting an adolescent to play an adolescent isn't after the event. They're still storming the Winter Palace and here are we expecting an objective historical report.

No question then about the most satisfactory solution. A total 'cheat' on age. A sixteen-year-old played by a youthful-looking actor in his early twenties. It can work remarkably well. To the point, in fact, at which your actual fifteen-year-old viewer will totally identify with them, as our correspondence reveals ('I feel that X must be just like me – could you send me his address'). The cheat can be further compounded by the technique of casting shortish boys and tallish girls. In boy-girl scenes this produces the image of nearly matching heights which we tend to associate with middle rather than late teens.

I must add that I detect occasionally a tendency in some teenage fiction to imply that characters are actually younger than their behaviour would lead you to suppose. Is this my own incipient middle-age or an attempt to hook as young a readership as possible? A few years back, Granada Television acquired an option on John Gordon's extraordinary novel *The House on the Brink*. For various reasons the project had to be shelved but a full location survey had been completed together with an eight-part adaptation so that we had got to know the book quite intimately. And something about the story just didn't fit. All the doors looked pretty tightly shut but there was still a draught. Following discussions with John Gordon we tried re-imagining hero and heroine a couple of years older and were delighted to find that without in the least disturbing the original 'line' of the novel, the crucial relationships between the young people and the adults had now suddenly 'found their place'.

The television production of *Flambards* involved an even more drastic decision. In the original trilogy, Christina first arrives at Flambards at the age of twelve. At the end of the third book she is around about twenty-two (exactly how many more months the First World War has left to run remains unspecified). By a curious coincidence this age-range is almost identical to that of the heroine of a BBC serialization running at about the same time, *The Mill on the Floss*. Like Christina Parsons, Maggie Tulliver moves from childhood to womanhood within some five hundred pages of narrative (rather closer spaced type in Maggie's case, I grant). Indeed, in *Reader's Digest* terms, the same paragraph might well summarize the plots of both books:

> In a rural setting, a strong-willed young girl grows up in the care of a headstrong and financially rash head of the house, whose heedless management of the family property has resulted in its mortgage. Amidst the problems to which this gives rise, the girl comes to womanhood via a series of complex relationships with the three principal young men in her life.

No actress could convincingly portray – over long and detailed scenes – an age range from twelve to her twenties (above all in close-up). The alternatives are either to re-write the story or gamble on finding a younger actress and an older actress to cover one and the same part. For *The Mill on the Floss* the BBC chose the latter course and pulled off a magnificent tour-de-force. For me, at least, in the transition from Georgia Slowe to Pippa Guard the quickness of director Paul Stone's hands had done everything that could be expected towards deceiving the eye.

In other respects, the adaptation was an altogether strange venture – five hundred pages of narrative reduced to four hours of screen time (contrast the *Flambards* trilogy which ran to eleven hours of screen time). But the innate precision in the casting of George Eliot's central character compelled a respect despite the almost outrageous sleight-of-hand with which events, characters and *sequiturs* were shed from the original novel.

By contrast, Mrs Peyton had agreed with Yorkshire Television that 'the time sequence should be condensed and the characters start at the age of roughly eighteen' (instead of twelve) 'for nobody wanted the immense difficulties of having to cope with child actors for several instalments and then change to adult actors'. (See Mrs Peyton's article in *Books for Your Children*, Winter 1978.)

Did it also perhaps cross someone's mind that a television series with a heroine of twelve years of age might be hard to sell to the rest of the network as a viable runner for an 8 p.m. transmission? Yes, I think it's a ploy I might have used as well!

But, despite the truncations, the BBC's two-actress Maggie did enable it to carry off one delicate prize – a sense of the shadows cast by the first footfalls down the corridor of adolescence. One remembers George Eliot's description of the moment when Maggie bids Mrs Stelling goodbye: 'the first sign . . . of that new sense which is the gift of sorrow'. Now the curious fact is that this incident never appeared in the BBC production, yet, because of our awareness of the full span of Maggie's growth, the *sense* of the moment was perfectly and poignantly present in the adaptation.

I must conclude the *Flambards–Floss* contrast where, in a sense, it started – the bookshop. In the summer of 1978, before any hint of television promotion for either novel, the one book (or trilogy) was stacked on the 'young fiction' shelves, the other along with established adult 'classics'. Comes their almost simultaneous transmission as television adaptations and both suddenly appear side by side on the 'current pushed line' display rack, all in paperback with colour stills from their respective television productions on the covers. The old catagories have suddenly disappeared. The new category for both, packaging 1860s and 1960s shoulder to shoulder is 'As Seen On Television'.

Now, the primary function of the television producer handling TFA is *not* to help sell books. Dear publisher, perhaps you should have been disabused of this idea a little earlier in this article. But equally, the primary function of your TF author, in setting pen to paper, is *not*, I trust, to make a fortune for a publishing house.

Nevertheless, what the television producer is about *has* got something to do with that strange new juxtaposition of styles and centuries on the bookshop display rack. To the majority of children who will never so much as open a work of fiction (other than a classroom reader) once they have left primary school, TFA is a world of blue touchpapers on unlabelled fireworks. And even after the television productions the vast, vast, majority still won't go near a bookshop even to notice those familiar television stills on the book covers.

But sitting in front of the television they might, yes, pick a firework at random. And of course there'll be a few damp squibs. But then, just occasionally (and depending of course on where you're standing at the time) there comes, all unexpectedly, this blazing core and a shower of sparks into the outer darkness which is something you had no label for but which was an illumination beyond belief. And it's as if you needed to trigger it again and again inside you (two thousand young people still compulsively run a corresponding society throughout this country about the television production of *The Prisoner*). And George Eliot might be John Rowe Townsend's son for all you know (there are so many names at the beginnings and ends of television shows) but Maggie's like a spark burning inside you because again and again you ask why does it have to happen like this to her? Does it *have* to happen? That was years ago surely. Years and years ago. Just like you this minute. So is it always going to happen like that? I mean, it starts out almost as if it was some sort of comedy . . .

The essence of all the very best TFA will be, must be, that it goes back to the original utterly idiosyncratic burn that was the gutniggle for that particular and singular author at that particular and singular time. You can't tamper with that. You can discard some of the trimmings, yes, but keep harping on the niggle. The niggle is what always comes through, however identical the glossy packaging. And what the very best of TFA offers in the end will always take the form of a question, hopefully never of a statement and unquestionably never of an answer.

And to hell with your messages. Television inundates us with people giving answers to questions. You might almost begin to think that for every question there *was* an answer. But no, answers are a debased currency. If you can't give an answer to my question, sir, within three seconds flat then you're either a political idiot or else a silly contestant who'll never win any of life's jackpots. Fahrenheit 481 is almost 450 degrees too high for the so-fair, so-necessary teenage social 'message' novels.

No, take a whole book to ask one bloody question and then maybe I'll listen, maybe I'll wonder. But give me an answer and I'll know you're a swindler and shouldn't be allowed near young people.

Which is why, on one desk at least, all books don't get the same equal chance, the same fair consideration. And why I, and I guess others, want, need and passionately desire to make an adaptation of one book rather than another. And what *The Owl Service* and *The Intruder* and *The House on the Brink* all offered in common: the question, what do these pictures really mean? Why does this white look black? Is it because it *is* black? In that case, why is it white? Or is it? And who is cheating whom? And who *thinks* he is cheating whom? And who is cheating because he's being so honest that it hurts? And why should it hurt? Why? Why? Don't ask *me*. Because I'm having to ask as well the whole time I'm working on the programme.

And here, landscape can be a maker or breaker. In the very best TF where it's organic to the structure of the story, a location can become, for a film director and cast, almost a kind of total *aide-memoire*, a summary of the main question. In making *The Owl Service* we had a major problem in that although we could use Garner's original mid-Wales valley as a location, the house within the valley that had been his inspiration was denied to us. But there are ways of wangling these effects of supposed juxtaposition and I acknowledge now as a major mistake my failure in the first five minutes of the film to tie the house's young trio to an overwhelming image of the valley, enclosed and enclosing, a crucible posing the question as to whether the ultimate explosion of the elements burning within it is inevitable.

Well, it's all a matter of learning by mistakes and when we came to make *The Intruder* a couple of years later, one of the features of John Rowe Townsend's book that especially excited us was precisely this link of landscape and character situation. Arnold Haithwaite, the hero of the book, is a Sand Pilot. His trade lies in his certainty of footstep across these vast shifting Cumbrian sandflats and channels. And yet, as his own personal certainties of identity begin to crumble, so the ironies attaching to this small pathfinder figure in his vast horizontal landscape increase. At the conclusion, all footholds give way completely. The landscapes of place and personal identity become simultaneously submerged in the final flood. Not dissimilar in fact, to the way Townsend later, in his *Summer People*, used the erosion of the cliff-house in the summer of 1939 to parallel both national and personal situations.

The novel not merely of question but of quest is, not unnaturally, always a likely candidate for serialization. Anticipation of the next length of search path is the bait for the next week's episode. And I have come to realize that the ideal is a very, very, simple basic search situation (whether for the significance of a legend, for one's own name or for the reason why a wooden post has moved – to use the Garner, Townsend and Gordon novels I have already mentioned) which offers the maximum time and space for the exploration of the ambiguities en route.

Like Alison in *The Owl Service*, tracing the plate patterns – necessity or wilfulness? Arnold in *The Intruder*, obsessionally becoming more Sonny than himself? Jane in the same book – looking at Arnold as if he were a human being or merely another mirror? And (would that we could have produced it!) Dick in *House on the Brink* – playing to win for his friends or merely using them as pieces to play with?

And every time, as I say, the question 'why?'

But, be warned, adults do not like ambiguities. I don't need to intrude on the privacy of our own viewers' mail for exemplars – the recent published correspondence in the *Radio Times* on the BBC's fascinating *Grange Hill* series was a public giveaway. 'Fair was foul and foul was fair – who was meant to be good and who was meant to be bad?' is a pretty basic summary of the cries of anguish.

Splendid.

You have your own adult television shows where the commentary will tell you the meaning of every picture and where the pundits will cure your heartache at a stroke.

Leave room for your children to see that some questions without answers can be major discoveries.

Part Three
The Readers

11 Who can teach reading?

Trevor Dickinson

October 1954. The room is bookless, bare of print. Tuesday. Sir Walter Scott. 2C, the third stream in the grammar school. 'Get out your *Lay of the Last Minstrels*', I say. (Should it have been 'Lays' I wonder?) This is the request every Tuesday afternoon second period – 'Layday'.

'Now where did we get to last week?' I ask. I have to ask since I can't recall. It's no mere test but probationary panic, a desperate, pennyfeathered hope that some boy will give an honest answer. They flick through their tired and battered copies of Scott (It was Scott, wasn't it?) and a boy calls out – even in those disciplined days – 'page 34, sir'. (It must have been Hulme: he went into educational publishing.)

'Right then' and I begin to read – what I still do not know – until the haze of October and last night's marking force lead upon my eyelids.

'Carry on, Cranston' – for twenty lines or so – 'Eason... Ewing... Home . . . Newman.'

'What was it all about?' I wonder now. What can any of it have meant to those bright boys then? What can they recall of it now? Little of pleasure I imagine.

October 1954. 4D sit in a similarly spartan room. It's Wednesday. *Romeo and Juliet* day. For the opinions they are about to receive (such as they are) may the Lord make them truly thankful. They've already had their dictated notes on Plot, Source and Treatment, Contrast, Coincidence, Detail, Atmosphere, Theme, Setting, The Masque, Dramatic Irony, Mood and Language. (Where did I get them from?) Today, a double period, we have playing of parts – the actors in their ranks of desks (Tybalt, could you be fiery? More passion, Thatcher!)

It's Act III Scene 1. After five lines I explain that Tybalt was the name for a cat – a fact dutifully noted, along with others, on and around the text.

'What's a pilchard? What does a sword go into?'

Ten volunteers.

'Croston?'

'Sir, a scabbard.'

'That's right, a scabbard. You wouldn't want a sword digging into your tights, would you?'

A tired laugh.

'What does he mean – "a grave man?" . . . "Zounds" where does that come from? I've mentioned that before. Does nobody remember? . . . What's a braggart? The first four letters should give you a clue.'

Seven minutes later we get back to the text.

' "Very friend" means "dear friend".'

And three lines later: ' "Aspired" means "has risen to the clouds"; "moe" means "more" . . .'

'Could we hear a little bit of anger and dismay all mixed in together, Hewitt . . .'

We cover 120 lines in 40 minutes.

'Well, that's a very important scene. Do you all see it's a turning point? For goodness' sake put your hand up if you don't? Is everybody with me?'

And so on to dictation (seventeen words a minute). 'Listen and don't forget. I can't speak when you're fidgeting. Well, I can but I'm not doing it. I'm sick and tired of telling you what similes and metaphors are. You ought to know. Well, for homework I want you to go through Act II and pick out some good imagery. Pick out some things you think are very attractive – the things that appeal to you. Then we'll go through them and see if you pick out the ones I think are the most obvious ones – the ones you could use in an exam. Now you're fidgeting again.'

May 1959. 5A. A small country grammar school. Environmental time has stood still as have the dictated chapter summaries of *Jane Eyre*. (I think I have them still?)

Even in 1967 ('I didn't get where I am today . . .') bright Sheila Metcalfe can, in the same setting, gain her November re-sit pass in O level English Literature with few glimmers of understanding. ('I just remembered all you told me,' she said). Moreover, she may, then an intending teacher, have left school believing that the whole of English Literature was contained in a handful of dusty poems,

Richard II and *The Mayor of Casterbridge.* To think that Professor Maurice Cranston reviewing George Steiner's *On Difficulty* in *The Sunday Times* in November 1978 should express the fear that 'the coming radical "reforms" of the Certificate of Education will ensure that in Great Britain the decay of learning will be discreetly veiled'.

As a teacher I was a slow learner. I taught Literature much as I had been taught it in my own grammar school days – too often with what Barrie Wade has called greater interest in pursuing a literary convention than in 'exploring the meanings of a poem' or a novel or a play. One major cause of sadness is the certain knowledge that the literary nit-picking approach, with its illusion of sharp deep scholarship, is slow and hard to lay to rest. In one sense, we did our job too well in the 1950s and 1960s – but at what cost in terms of developing the joyful enthusiasm of those who might otherwise have learned 'to read fully?' For just as there seems little doubt that the one common feature shared by adult illiterates is their failure to realize that reading was a source of pleasure for others, so our most able readers must have been similarly deprived by the soullessness of our approach.

My own teaching experience offers me small consolation. Recently, in Grimsby, I met Martin Bartlett – whom I'd not seen since I taught him in that first grammar school. I sought to mumble apologetically about the damage I'd done him – assuring him (Why? And was it true, anyway?) that I was better when I finished teaching in 1968. He didn't (as I had, I am sure hoped) insist that I was a first-rate teacher. But I did take warm delight (the glow still there) from his reminder – 'It was you who read us *Crime and Punishment* when I was in the sixth form. I can remember that.' The memory offers some sliver of hope. Martin had retained something of that frenzied hotch-potch of my enthusiasm for reading and especially for reading aloud to youngsters. (How did my enthusiasm grow? Certainly not from my limited literature schooling. Not from university. Perhaps from my father's own storytelling? Perhaps from the drama work Dennis Fielder and Arthur Pickett started at school on their return from war service?) As I write now I recall at random some of the names whose works I read – all four divisions represented plus some who wouldn't even have been admitted to the League. Oscar Wilde (I gave my copy of *Reading Gaol* to Gary in 1964 on his promise that he would read it once a year. Did he, I wonder?) A. G. Macdonell, Leacock, Joyce, Dylan Thomas, Hemingway, Greene, Parker, Frost, Hopkins, Wordsworth, Sillitoe, Thurber, Perelman, Runyan, Bradbury, Hughes – and so on.

That kind of purposeful indiscrimination is happily still to be seen (although, for me, there are today some limits: non-censorship may lead to the subtler censorship of the market place). It is the kind of indiscrimination upon which sharper, more perceptive selection ultimately depends. In one sense, that is, there is a false distinction drawn by Professor Cranston between 'the fun syllabus' and 'the art of serious reading'. So now the heavily 'adult' flavour of the names dropped in my last paragraph needs to be supplemented in the lower and middle years of the secondary school by the presence of Lively, Garfield, Dahl, Fox, Byars, Mark, Westall, O'Brien, Rowe Townsend, Aiken, Treece, the Cleavers, Southall, Garner, Vance Marshall, Boston, Pearce, Mayne, Sutcliff, Ashley, Paton Walsh, Everard Palmer, Causley, Walsh, Kit Wright, Milligan and so very many more – again from all divisions.

Good literature teaching depends to large extent upon bulk – and upon the blessing of the paperback, so directly appealing that its short life can be partly forgiven. (Better the eagerly devoured 'Rabbiting on' than a shelf of 'Minstrels' still taking unread space!) It depends too upon wise buying of that bulk. That in turn means a teaching staff (not merely the English department) knowing more about what is available to be read to and by their children, and being, in consequence, less dependent upon distantly produced lists and catalogues. Where literature is most successfully handled it is in those schools where there is a pretty close awareness by teachers of how particular books will 'speak to particular children at the right time'. This awareness depends upon teachers reading what is being published (again, not merely teachers of English). Good book policy for a school depends upon wide reading.

Again, where literature has life in a school, it is in that school which sees the possibility of a variety of approaches. So there are large sets for whole class treatment; there are smaller sets of five or six copies of identical title; there are single copies for individual, private reading. Certainly, where literature flourishes there are books on display in classrooms and libraries – even in otherwise bleak corridors. In an increasing number of schools there is the display of books (and posters and articles and reviews) to be found in the school bookshop. These, now sometimes run by parent volunteers (not volunteer parents!) are always at their best when they shun the atmosphere of a decaying bolt-hole and seek a positive style. Reading is a somewhat private activity that does not always find a 'natural' home in the public place of the school. The good school bookshop – or library – is that which takes the hallowed air from the activity and makes for easy, informal but committed exchange about books. It is sometimes the happy centre for a 'Reading club'.

That exchange about books like so much else in schools depends upon the teacher. That truism needs stating. All too often schools are blamed for the inadequacies of their charges. All too rarely are they encouraged to realize their positive power. Thus the supply of books in schools – in terms of both quantity and quality – is a telling shaper of children's attitudes towards books and the act and art of reading. Similarly the 'easy, informal, committed exchange' hinges upon good teaching. There are important external factors. The 'right' examination syllabus and approach can encourage good practice and a growth of reading desire. The 'wrong' examination is likely to do little but alienate – and its backwash will leave tedious tidemarks on the lower reaches of the school. None the less, however good the exam, it will not compensate for poor teaching. Good teaching, on the other hand, can compensate to some degree for a limited and limiting examination course.

Good literature teaching is that which ensures no sad division between literature for 'study' and literature for 'pleasure'. In the best of schools, good literature teaching encourages work in a variety of modes. It makes use of the informal and the extracurricular such as the Reading club earlier mentioned, with occasional visits by readers – other teachers, older pupils, retired teachers, advisers, local college staff, staff and students from other schools, parents and so on. Within the classroom, it gives children the chance to share the same book as a class and with peers in a group, or to make independent choices – perhaps later to be shared with a group or the class. The important feature of the best practice is the happy chance it gives to children (and here the ghost of my early teaching shakes to fading!) to bring their responses to books and to be less dependent upon the received opinion prescribed by the teacher.

This means that time and space are (have to be) made available for the hesitant articulation and exchange of points of view, for those uncertainty-reducing questions by children that, in general, are too infrequently found in our schools. It means that the environment and the very arrangement of the furniture, are (have to be) seen as vital contributors to the dialogue style. It does *not* mean that the teacher opts out. Again, although much talk about books and plays and poems will, in good schools, take place without the teacher eagerly at the child's shoulder, his presence earlier will have been vital in enabling the child to learn how to contribute helpfully to profitable talk. In some schools children can benefit from seeing (or hearing on tape) their own teachers talking together critically about literature. Without good guidance from teachers the small group discussion of a poem can become an irritatingly painful blind alley. Good teaching and good example lead to generosity of tone, unforced reflection, and, in the long run, greater enthusiasm and sharpness of critical perception.

Reading and talking about what is read are, however, only two aspects of literature teaching to be found in the successful classroom.

A third aspect I have already touched upon – that of reading aloud to children. A good department is that which gives high priority to this activity – particularly, of course, in mixed ability classes where, otherwise, some children may not yet have for themselves the skills to cope with certain texts. In the highest of streamed classes there is a case for reading aloud when the ablest readers may still be needing the model of the teacher's ability to 'lift the text off the page'. But where children have difficulty with reading they need, even more especially, as Margaret Clark has pointed out, to hear written language orally presented – live or on tape. Without this, such children experience an ever-widening gap between what they can read and what, in a sense, they need to be able to read. It is important in this context for teachers to ask themselves: 'If I don't read to my children, who will?'

There is a fourth aspect of good literature teaching which demands attention, this, too, one which is seen in successful schools to have a bearing on all children whatever their diagnosed level of ability. It concerns what has been called the Creative response. From the child's earliest days in school it does seem that so much time is spent on comprehension exercises. As the child grows older and reaches the middle years of secondary school he meets an increasing quantity of such work in various guises across the curriculum. Keen-sighted English teachers, however, have become increasingly aware of the fact that creative interpretation of text (again, 'lifting text off the page') is a more powerful, attractive and worthwhile means of demonstrating understanding. It involves, of course, being able to dig beneath the surface of the author's intention.

With this in mind, some schools are giving children more chances to give life to print – through dramatization of text, live or taped, for presentation to real audiences within and beyond the school. They are giving chances too for the creative response evidenced in the act and art of making their own literature. Sometimes this involves 'original' writing or the retelling of some familiar story, perhaps for a younger audience. Sometimes it involves writing for the self, the group or the class. Sometimes there is a wider audience in mind for the children's own literary creation. Again, the best literature here grows from encounters with the models of a rich range of literature by adults (and other children). It grows from sensitive discussion of the child's work – by teacher and other children.

Of course, such creative activity, especially when the impact of the art upon real audiences can be brought home to young writers, is important, not merely because of its contribution to the child as maker. As far as the teaching of literature is concerned it is also one vital means whereby the child is able to express his critical response to what he reads. It is, moreover, an important means of enlarging the child's critical understanding and appreciation of the writer's craft.

There is much more that might have been said. I have chosen not to argue the case for literature as beneficial to the child's development – although I do believe with Graham Greene that, in the first fourteen years of life, books do influence the future. I have chosen not to stress the importance of folk-tale, fantasy, myth and legend in giving children a sense of the permanence of human experience in terms of time and place. I have chosen not to develop Ezra Pound's argument that 'Literature is news that stays news'. I have consciously decided not to pursue my belief that imaginative literature has an important part to play in developing children's wider understanding of the world about them and that, in consequence, it ought to have wider use across the curriculum. I have said nothing about the value of seeking in schools to make more positive use of literature as presented on television – a powerful force for promoting reading. And there is so much more that might have been said about the profitable use of audiovisual aids.

There are only two more things I want to set down. The first is the valuable healthy reminder given by Nobel prize-winner, Isaac Bashevis Singer, in a recent newspaper article.

> Children read books, not reviews. Children don't read to find their identity, to free themselves from guilt, to quench the thirst for rebellion or to get rid of alienation. They have no use for psychology. They detest sociology. They still believe in God, the family, angels, devils, witches, goblins, logic, clarity, punctuation, and other such obsolete stuff. They love interesting stories, not commentaries, guides or footnotes. When a book is boring, they yawn openly. They don't expect their writer to redeem humanity, but leave to adults such childish illusions.

The last word must be given to my imaginary poet-philosopher, Pertwee Rumboldt, whose question makes clear, I hope, the essential prerequisite for happily successful teaching and learning of literature.

'Who can teach reading who does not himself love books?'

12 'Sir, why do you make it so boring?'
David Burns

I had been teaching a couple of years, perhaps, when my breathtaking exegesis of *Lord of the Flies* was interrupted by a pleasant, quiet girl in 5R – my O Lit. group. 'Sir, why do you make it so boring?' was all she said – pleasantly, quietly. I do not remember now how I reacted, though I hope with none of the savagery my wounded pride must have felt, for it remains the most bitter and salutory lesson of my teaching career. The accusation was clear: the boredom was generated by me, not the text. It is a pity, perhaps, that we do not actively seek such consumer-reaction more frequently for such chance moments of painful honesty inevitably lead to reassessment. Life in large urban comprehensive schools smacks little enough of the fairy tale – and certainly I cannot claim that those particular magic words broke the spell that had held me in thrall and transformed me into one of the intuitive great teachers of literature that seem to appear so regularly as touchstones in the biographies of our Grand Old Men of Letters, generating an unquenchable thirst for books. Nevertheless, the shame bred of that moment returns often enough to keep me worrying about teenage reading: asking how we may best foster a love of reading which will survive the shredding of set books; seeking ways in which continued reading for pleasure and the demands of public examinations may be reconciled; searching for ways in which we may continue teaching and not merely putting books in front of children.

It barely needs stating, I suppose, but we ought to be clear that this is no paper tiger. Whatever our experience might have led us to believe, Frank Whitehead's research must come as a surprise to a few, an unwelcome confirmation to many – and a shattering condemnation of us all. ('Children and their Books'; Schools Council Research Studies; Macmillan Education.) There cannot be an English syllabus in the country that does not mention in some form the encouragement of children's personal reading amongst its aims.

And yet amongst the 14+ age group 36 per cent of all children (and 40 per cent of all 14+ boys) were doing no book-reading at all in their leisure time during the period of the research. It is worth adding that over half of those were assessed by their teachers as average or above average in general school attainment and so belong to the 'won't read' rather than 'can't read' category. Similarly a study by G. Yarlott and W. S. Harpin ('1,000 responses to English Literature' *Educational Research* 13.1 and 13.2: 1972/73) revealed that of 1,000 O and A level literature students a mere 170 had any intention of reading any poetry once they had left school. What price the avowals of the departmental guidelines we have all been party to which have the declared aim of stimulating an appreciation of poetry?

This gulf between our stated aims and the reality of what we actually achieve is always going to exist, of course. Despite our best efforts, we will always fail in some measure to produce school-leavers able 'to write correctly, coherently and imaginatively' or able 'to speak fluently in an appropriate register' to quote a couple of fairly typical syllabus aims I have seen recently. I suspect, however, that the gulf is nowhere wider, the abyss nowhere deeper than in the area of the teaching of literature and the promotion of reading for pleasure. Is it unfair to suggest that the majority of literature teaching is actually of the kind which leads directly to the non-reading figures revealed by Whitehead's survey? That the very methods and texts we employ to teach literature are in large measure themselves responsible for the rejection and boredom we have all observed?

By the time children are in to the third year of secondary school we seem to have lost sight of the pleasure principle which is the bedrock upon which all more sophisticated responses to reading are based. Suddenly life becomes serious and children only come into contact with books as sources of information, inexhaustible funds of problems to be solved, disjoint plundered extracts to be comprehended or set texts to be anatomized, digested and regurgitated to order. As teachers, we find it hard to shake off our own traditional academic lit. crit. backgrounds; it comes all too easily and naturally to offer up to all our pupils a watered-down critical method possibly appropriate to only a small minority. Even for them, much of our current approach merely produces the stereotyped response, the inability to think creatively for oneself, the blithe acceptance of other

people's interpretations about all of which teachers in higher education complain. Like all English teachers my marking of O and A
level essays has been punctuated by sighs of irritation at my students'
seeming inability to go beyond what I had already suggested or what
was encapsulated in the commercial study notes. And yet what more
did I deserve, could I reasonably have expected, not having given
these same youngsters a chance over the years to build a background
for orienting their own reactions and judgments? My own anxious-
ness that they should be producing some kind of critical analytic
response to their reading tended to produce the very stereotypes I
was hoping to see diminish as they became more experienced. The
freshness and honesty one might reasonably have expected from
intelligent adolescents had been bred out of them, their capacity for
responding openly to the work as a whole had been stunted by that
over-detailed nit-picking brand of literary criticism which is still the
common diet.

The Examination Boards, of course, have a case to answer here.
Most cling stubbornly to an analysis and heritage model which
allows precious little scope for the imaginative study of more
accessible modern works; or they offer a syllabus which tempts a
teacher into covering the minimum number of texts in the maximum
pleasure-destroying detail; or they set ludicrous questions; or . . . the
arguments have been well-rehearsed and need no further repetition.
Yet it is idle to pretend that alternatives do not exist. The department
which is really dissatisfied and feels restricted by examination con-
straints has open to it other more liberal boards and the possibilities
offered by Mode 3. The fact that so large a majority of departments
are content to rumble on with the *status quo* is a condemnation of
us as teachers, not the Boards. Growth and change will only come
with pressure from the teaching profession and, sadly, I believe that
the will to work for such change is lacking. How else could it be
that one so often finds literature as an option in years four and five
to allow the less able to spend longer practising those language skills
they have already spent ten years at school failing to master?

Too many of us have lost sight of the fact that we want youngsters
'to read for themselves, widely, voraciously and indiscriminately'
and that that process has its basis in enjoyment, for 'true personal
discrimination or taste develops slowly and probably best uncon-
sciously. It cannot be forced by exercises in selecting the good and

rejecting the bad, by the application of stock critical formulas: it may indeed be stunted. It comes, if it is to come at all, by growth in understanding and enjoyment of the good.' (Helen Gardner *The Business of Criticism;* OUP.)

Mode 3 CSE in particular has offered us an opportunity to match our teaching to our avowed aims of encouraging the children's personal reading, of building on the pleasure principle, but too many of us have failed to take it. On the other hand I know schools where O lit. has been totally abandoned to make maximum use of the greater scope offered by Mode 3 CSE. This has enabled those departments to make the examination the logical combination of a coherent five-year course which has placed books and reading at the heart of its teaching. (I hesitate even to say 'literature' for it always has the mystique-laden whiff of a capital L about it.) Having spent years one to three encouraging extensive reading in a variety of ways they have seen the inherent nonsense of suddenly spending the next two years on a painstaking grind through possibly as few as three set texts and have opted for an examination heavily weighted towards course work. Certainly they have recognized the importance of some intensive study and Shakespeare, Dickens, Hardy, Lawrence and Orwell still represent set authors. Certainly, too, the traditional lit. crit. analytical essay still has its place – but often in a stimulating and logical form as, say, a single long essay written over a couple of weeks with access to the text, notes and any criticism the candidate cares to make use of. Some schools have also devised methods of assessing oral work, to be taken into account alongside each long essay, so that each pupil's contributions in group and class discussion may be given some weight. Pupils are given a further opportunity to clarify points, made perhaps uncertainly in their essays, by a short *viva voce* with their teacher following the initial marking.

Some schools have recognized that reading is partly a matter of habit and realized their responsibility for fostering that habit for as long as possible; to help sustain the sheer volume of reading they have devised syllabuses which give credit for both quantity and quality for personal reading. The same schools often tend to build into their syllabuses some form of individual project of a literary nature which may vary widely from the study of war through novels, war comics and personal creative writing, to the creation of a child's picture book, to an analysis of an author or genre, to a comparison of women's/teenage magazines and so on. Such flexibility allows young people to start where they currently are, often to legitimize their own leisure reading even if it is of a non-book kind. The point is that such flexibility tries to build on a department's previous work, recognizes the huge range of individual responses to reading and seeks to encourage and broaden rather than deaden and restrict.

And what about language work, I hear you all shouting. A literature-based course of this kind certainly tends to be very time-consuming, dominating some two-thirds of the year's work. I can only state my belief that language competence grows when language is used with interest and enthusiasm in some kind of real context. The kind of course I have outlined certainly generates an atmosphere within which language use can flourish – and I doubt whether I could say the same about most of my course-book based language teaching. At least it is true that O and CSE language results improved – though only a little – with the introduction of a reading-based course which included most of the elements outlined above. It is worth adding that in my experience such preparation has tended to produce A level candidates with a far wider reading experience, an open-mindedness and freshness unsullied by the inappropriate cramming process typical of much O lit. teaching.

Returning to the 'coherent policy' and moving down the school, it seems to me that it is precisely the lack of such a policy that leads to the rather aimless random approach to reading for pleasure which characterizes so much of our English teaching. Somehow, whatever we may say to the contrary in our declared aims, encouraging reading, helping children to become life-long readers, is merely peripheral – a chance by-product of the 'real work' of an English department. Thus we do not actually set out with the intention of making books enjoyable. Even a class-reader used with a first-year group risks being subjected to a whole range of pedagogic abuses including vocabulary testing, spelling, inane comprehension, 'hearing them read', and what Aidan Chambers has aptly called 'grammatical rape'. All of which may or may not improve understanding but will undoubtedly destroy a book's potential as a source of pleasure. Likewise visits to the library – always assuming that it is not being used for fifth year careers or as the offenders' centre – are too often dominated by Dewey, catalogues and learning to retrieve information. (I cannot really see why we bother since we are in so many other ways actively ensuring that the same youngsters will have little enough desire to go near a library once we have finished with them.)

I am not suggesting that all those aspects of English teaching are unimportant. Nor do I subscribe to the notion that the text is sacrosanct, that it will always speak for itself; nor the view that simply putting a child and book together and allowing some marvellous alchemical action to do the rest is always sufficient – though it can be. I do suggest, though, that we need to ask ourselves about the purpose of reading books with children. As part of that process – undertaken over a period of departmental discussion, say, we should look hard and long at the nature of the response we demand from young readers. It seems inevitable that one outcome should be a realization that there must be some element of intelligent risk on our part. The risk, of course, lies in encouraging children to find their own ways of responding to their reading in the first instance; in devising strategies and tasks which deliberately weaken our traditional dominant position as, say, the lynchpin of discussion; strategies which recognize that children will take from a novel of any depth those things which are currently of moment to them; strategies which begin to explore the close relationship of interpretative and creative activities. The re-working of a short story into the form of a radio play, for example, would seem to demand comprehension skills of the highest order, while re-writing a particular scene from a novel with a shifted viewpoint would demand an understanding of character far deeper than that elicited by those dreadful notes on characterization. In other words, a shift away from the tightly controlled teacher directed analytic response does not automatically lead to a vacuous *laissez-faire* approach lacking intellectual rigour. It is simply that interpretation in the fullest sense may often be best expressed creatively and that a response of this kind will allow a book to survive as a source of pleasure in a way which much of our traditional teaching, cerebral and schematized, cannot hope to do. We spend so much time teaching children the names and functions of leaves and trees that we blind them and desensitize them to the beauty and excitement to be found in the wood as a whole. It is not within the scope of this article to explore in detail these approaches which may both support and deepen a young reader's intuitive felt response. Readers who would like to delve further are urged to read

Patterns of Language (Stratta, Dixon and Wilkinson; HEB) which is an excellent book and has a fascinating chapter on literature and interpretation.

The work of the Leeds NATE Group on the Schools Council 'Children as Readers' Project gives us further evidence for believing that we must endure the risk of abdicating *some* of our teaching for the sake of the pupils' learning. In an important article in *English in Education* (5; 3 – Winter 71) they report on the successes (and limitations) of their experiments with the undirected group discussion of a novel. They found that, particularly in the early stages of developing a response to a novel, small groups worked remarkably successfully and concluded that an ideal situation would start with undirected group work leading on to full-class discussion where the teacher's experience could operate more effectively once initial responses had been focused, ideas rehearsed and so on. Two key sentences in the Group's article linger for me: 'At times we felt that some of the natural animation of the playground had come into classroom learning. It is this kind of energy and self-confidence in exploring literature that we all wish to encourage.' (Another guilty shudder as I think of 5R!)

And so back to our coherent policy. Not only does a department need an examination which is the logical outcome of a course leading up to it but it needs to have collectively considered the nature of the responses it expects and to have taught accordingly throughout the school. Thus the introduction of group-talk suddenly in year four at random by individual teachers is not likely to prove very effective. Similarly there needs to be an understood commitment of time to reading: too often the set-book is solemnly dragged reluctantly from desks for its thirty-five minute weekly airing when it might benefit from continuous reading from cover to cover in successive English lessons. I know many teachers who feel instinctively that such an approach might make sense on occasion but who are guilt stricken at not having administered the weekly dose of comprehension or who are afraid of being seen reading aloud to the class. ('Again, Mrs Jones? Surely that is the second time this week I have seen you reading aloud to 2S. They're not at junior school now, you know.') Quite why this is an activity deemed suitable only for young children I cannot imagine. Reading aloud remains one of the most effective means of ensuring that a novel is enjoyed and understood. The BBC would hardly waste so much air-time on the many story readings for adults were it merely a childish pastime.

This need not merely be an English department commitment either: I see no reason why secondary schools should not introduce the practice of some primary schools in starting each day with a session of free-reading for all – from the head down. Children, after all, have little enough evidence that their teachers actually read for pleasure and I suspect this is simply because we do not read enough; or when we do, we do not spend enough time sharing our reactions to books with children. We certainly do not read enough of the same material that children read and without that we cannot communicate shared pleasures, enthusiasms and disappointments about individual titles and authors, we cannot help children's reading to develop by knowing where to direct them next, we cannot generate enthusiasm and interest in new additions to the library stock. (On what basis were they bought, anyway, if nobody has read them or at least read a review independent of the publisher's catalogue blurb?) We would all look askance at the car salesman who knew next to nothing about his product and did not feel particularly enthusiastic about it one way or the other anyway. One sentence from the evidence to the Bullock Committee rings in my ears like a death-knell. Talking of pupils admitted to an adult literacy scheme it was said of their failure to learn to read: 'Only one common factor emerges: they did not learn from the process of learning to read that it was something other people did *for pleasure.*' Is an illiterate merely someone who cannot read; or may he also be someone who can, but has never actually been motivated to do so beyond a purely functional level? Our responsibility either way seems clear enough.

In terms of coherent policy, then, two further points emerge. In giving reading for pleasure the proper commitment of time within the curriculum we must ensure that it is matched by our own professional commitment. We must ensure that we ourselves are readers and that we know the books. Life is hectic and keeping up with new publications difficult which means sharing the reading within the department, holding regular departmental oral reviewing sessions when each may talk about a couple of books read over the past few weeks, ensuring that newspaper reviews and specialist review-journals are circulated, passing on information about children's reactions to specific books, discussing the successes and failures of particular approaches to specific class-readers and so on. Secondly, we must record each child's reading consistently. Ideally such a record should pass on with each child from his junior school and then be continued in some form throughout his whole life. It should include books, magazines, comics, newspapers read at home as well as those found at school. It is not a particularly arduous task – especially if kept by the child on some kind of pro forma – and it will always provide us with a means of assessing the development of a pupil's reading, give us a basis for discussion with each child and thereby encourage growth. Aidan Chambers in *Introducing Books to Children* (Heinemann Educational Books) and Christopher Walker in *Reading Development and Extension* (Ward Lock Educational) both offer detailed advice on reading records. Suffice it to say that such records reduce the chance element in the pattern of a child's reading and above all they are clear proof to children that we care about reading for pleasure, that it merits careful thought and discussion.

Until we really begin to take it seriously, to show our enthusiasm and belief by a commitment of time and resources, by professional discussion of aims and methods which reflect an active policy for the promotion of reading for pleasure, there is little chance that our pupils will make the same commitment. The role of bookshops, central and classroom libraries, class readers, book promotion, are all part of that discussion along with the issues raised earlier and must all be considered for the part they have to play in any such policy. We must find answers to the challenges thrown out by Whitehead's research and consider their implications for our attitudes and approaches in school. What conclusions are we to draw from the high correlation of book-ownership and commitment to reading; of heavy periodical reading and heavy book reading? What of the apparently adverse effects upon voluntary reading in schools which provided course books, comprehension books and thematic anthologies? How are we going to respond to the team's serious doubts about 'the adequacy and suitability of the book provision made in school and class libraries' and their view that 'many schools need to allocate more of their resources to the purchase of such books (i.e. those suitable for leisure-time reading) and to develop more expertise in their selection'?

Above all we must work towards departmental commitment so that the drive is not coming from an isolated individual but from a team generating enthusiasm for books which is all pervasive. Talking about the number of schools where the reading-habit has been successfully established the interim report of Whitehead's research says:

> In each case the principal influence was that of a teacher or librarian who was himself a keen reader and therefore prepared to take seriously the development of children's reading. If this kind of conviction and dedication were more widespread we are convinced that the incidence of non-book-readers among the age range we studied would soon be reduced to an insignificant proportion (Schools Council Working Paper 52).

Amen to that.

13 Developing and extending the reading habit
John L. Foster

In recent years the concern to improve standards of reading among secondary school pupils has led to a reappraisal of the methods being used to develop the higher skills of reading. The traditional comprehension exercise, with its series of questions, varying in type and difficulty from those concerned with the meanings of individual words to inferential questions about the author's intentions, is still as widely used as ever. However, its limitations are enormous. Even the most skilled questioner cannot hope to predict the exact nature of each individual's response to what he has read. It is, therefore, impossible to draw up a set of questions that will help every reader to full comprehension. Consequently, an increasing number of teachers have begun to use alternative methods, such as exercises involving cloze procedure, group prediction or group sequencing.

The aim of any school's reading policy must be to help pupils to learn to read efficiently, critically and habitually. Exercises designed to develop efficient reading, by improving comprehension abilities, have an integral part to play in such a policy. Yet, the keystone of such a policy must be the development of the individual's personal reading interests. Exercises can help a pupil to develop the higher reading skills and to become a more efficient reader. Literature study can help him to learn the techniques and language of criticism and to become a more critical reader. But it is the pupil's own reading that helps him to develop the reading habit.

The need to concentrate on the development of the reading habit cannot be over stressed. In our advanced technological age the written word retains its importance. Books remain one of the primary sources of information and ideas in our society. They continue, too, to provide many people with hours of enjoyment. If pupils are to leave school ready to turn to books for information and for pleasure during their adult lives, then the reading habit must be fostered during their schooldays.

There are other reasons why the development of the reading habit should be central to a school's reading policy. It is acknowledged by English teachers that those pupils who read widely have a greater command of language than those children of equal ability, who are not such avid readers. Also, it is as true of secondary school pupils, as it is of primary school pupils, that children learn to read by reading. The more a teenager reads, the more discerning a reader he becomes. The value of group discussion activities, cloze procedure exercises and literature study tasks is that they augment and broaden the critical awareness and efficiency in reading that a child develops through his own wide reading.

The chief priority in any secondary-school reading programme must, therefore, be the provision of time for individual personal reading. It is not sufficient merely to provide ten minutes, once a week, at the end of a lesson for pupils to go to the library to change their books. There needs to be time for actual reading, as well as for the choosing of books. How vital it is for a substantial block of time to be made available for personal silent reading is made only too clear by the report of the Schools Council Effective Use of Reading project. Their research findings show that the average time spent on uninterrupted reading in most secondary school lessons is under two minutes. It appears that, in many schools, the regular opportunity for a sustained period of reading rarely occurs, even in English lessons.

The way that textbooks are often used in the secondary-school classroom is surely one of the reasons why there is a decline in the number of children who read books, during the secondary school years. To counteract the deleterious effect that such a use of books has on the attitude of many teenagers towards books in general, there should, ideally, be several periods of time each week set aside for individual reading. However, the demands of subject specialists, preoccupied with covering the syllabus in order to prepare pupils for examinations, influence the construction of the secondary school timetable to such an extent that in only a few enlightened schools does reading appear on the timetable. But in those schools where reading is separately timetabled the teachers report a considerable improvement not only in the pupils' attitude towards books, but also in their reading ability and their general academic performance.

In most schools, however, it is left to the English department to draw up a reading policy and to provide time, from within the timetable allocation for English, for individual reading. In practice this often means that a half-hour or an hour per week is devoted to reading in the lower secondary school. Some CSE candidates may be fortunate enough to enjoy a weekly reading period throughout the fourth and fifth years, but in many schools the pressures of preparing pupils for CSE and GCE examinations mean that the reading period disappears at some point during these two years. The case for retaining the reading period throughout the fourth and fifth years is, however, a strong one, for such evidence as there is – from those teachers who have been bold enough not to dispense with it – suggests that their candidates' examination results have not suffered in any way. Indeed, there are claims that a widely based reading programme enables candidates to achieve higher grades.

One way of ensuring that all pupils get an opportunity for individual reading at least once a week is to arrange for a tutor group period to be utilized in this way. During tutor group time the tutor often has a number of administrative chores to perform. It takes a lot of preparation and considerable expertise to arrange activities that will hold the attention of a mixed-ability tutor group, and will enable the tutor to complete his administrative work uninterrupted. In consequence, tutor group time, in many schools, is not very effectively used. Designating one tutor group period per week to be spent by all the pupils in the school on individual reading, not only helps the development of the reading habit. It has the added advantages of relieving tutors of the burden of preparation for that period, and of involving all teachers – whatever their subject specialisms – in the implementation of the school's reading policy.

Obviously, the more the whole staff can be involved in encouraging pupils to read, the more successful the school's reading policy is likely to be. Providing time for individual reading is the first essential. It is also necessary to make an adequate provision of books. If we are to interest all the pupils in the school in reading, then we must provide a wide range of books, of varying degrees of difficulty.

Our chief criterion in choosing books for the school library and the class library must be whether or not the books will appeal to the young reader. This does not mean that we should totally disregard the quality of the books. Rather, it means that the quality of the books should be a secondary consideration, and that the first questions we must ask ourselves when making our selection are: will pupils want to read this book? Will it hold their interest? Will they enjoy it?

Nor does it mean that we should spend all our capitation allowance filling the shelves with Mills and Boon romances, Starsky and Hutch books, and biographies of football and pop stars. But we would be burying our heads in the sand if we did not acknowledge that such books exist and that many teenagers read them. If we are to interest those who are often categorized as reluctant readers in books and to help them to develop the reading habit, then we must be prepared to make concessions to their tastes. The last fifteen years have seen a tremendous expansion in the publication of books specifically designed to appeal to the uncommitted reader. Many of them have proved extremely popular and we do the reluctant teenage reader a disservice, if we are unwilling to countenance offering him such books, on the grounds that they are of an inferior literary quality.

The aim of a school's reading policy must be, however, not only to get all the pupil's reading, but also to extend their reading interests. Getting a pupil to read more widely can sometimes prove as difficult as getting him to read at all. Even in schools where there is a successful reading policy, and a great deal of individual reading takes place, there will be some pupils who never progress further than the undemanding stories by such authors as Dianne Doubtfire, Jean Saunders and Michael Hardcastle. Yet, there are many others who, once their interest in books has been aroused, can be helped to extend the range of their reading, if there is a wide enough selection of books. Ideally, there needs to be a massive variety of titles, if the needs of all pupils are to be met. In practice, a selection from the M Books, Heinemann New Windmill, Topliner Redstar, Puffin and Peacock series, will provide a range of titles, with a wide appeal, that will extend the reading of many pupils.

The role of the teacher in extending children's reading interests is important. By keeping a check on what each individual is reading, the teacher can know the type of books that interest a particular pupil and be in a position to recommend appropriate titles. Skilled intervention by a teacher suggesting the right book at the right moment can be a significant factor in helping a pupil to discover a new author or to find other books similar to, but slightly more demanding than, those he has previously enjoyed. If the record of each individual's reading is kept on a card, the cards can easily be passed on, when a class changes its teacher and the new teacher can see at a glance exactly what each pupil's reading interests are.

Such cards serve a dual purpose, for they also provide a record of the books borrowed from the class library. Unless a systematic check of such loans is kept, the stock will rapidly become depleted and, because of a lack of books, it may become difficult to maintain the pupils' enthusiasm for reading. One of the best ways of ensuring that books are returned regularly is to hold the reading lesson at the same time each week. This makes it easier for the pupils to remember when to bring their reading books to school.

However, when we consider the question of returning borrowed books, it is worth remembering that few of us are paragons of virtue. The system of loaning books from the school library needs to be flexible enough to tolerate some abuse. Otherwise it will almost certainly penalize those very pupils whom we have to cajole into taking a book out. Of course, we must not allow pupils to borrow books and never return them. But too rigid a system of fines and suspensions for those with overdue books can be counter-productive. It may only serve to alienate, and act as such a deterrent that the offender stops using the library altogether.

But the teacher's role involves more than just talking to teenagers, recommending titles, issuing books and recording what each individual is reading. It involves the organization of activities designed to stimulate wide reading. Book clubs, book fairs and a school bookshop can all play a part. So too can the skilled use of class readers, the reading of extracts from books which teenagers might enjoy, or a lesson devoted to going through a reading list.

Another effective way of creating and extending interest is to organize activities in which the pupils share their reading experiences. The most obvious method is to get each pupil to give a short talk to the class about a favourite book and to read an extract from it. This is a worthwhile activity, but can prove less successful than the teacher hoped, because many teenagers lack the expertise required to prepare and present a talk that will hold the attention of all their classmates. An alternative is to ask the class to work in groups and to prepare a tape-recording in which they talk about the books they have been reading and present extracts from them. Any particularly successful tape-recordings can then be played not only to their own class, but to other classes as well. But even if the final tape-recording does not reach that standard – and in most cases it probably won't! – the process of sharing their experiences is beneficial to the members of the group.

Another alternative is the book forum. A group of pupils with similar reading interests choose two or three titles – perhaps books by the same author, books in a particular series, or books in the same genre, e.g. science fiction. Having read the books, they present a discussion of the books in front of the class and answer questions about them. Book forums can be organized to assess the appeal of books which the teacher is considering purchasing either for class use or for the class library.

Throughout the secondary school pupils should also be encouraged to write reviews of the books that they have read. Every effort should be made to make this a meaningful activity, by providing as wide a readership as possible for the reviews. In some areas, the schools library service or local branch of the School Library Association have undertaken the production of booklets of reviews, written by pupils in local schools, copies of which have been circulated to schools and public libraries. The school's reprographic equipment can be used to produce duplicated review sheets for distribution within the school, and a section of any creative writing, or school, magazine can be reserved for reviews. At the very least, handwritten copies of reviews can be mounted on sugar paper and displayed as broadsheets on the classroom walls.

An annual reviewing competition can be organized with a prize for the best review in each year group, as well as an overall prize. This will have the most widespread effect if all the pupils are expected to enter and if it is linked to a book event of some kind. For example, a week may be designated Book Week. A book fair can be organized and an author invited to speak. There can be a short story competition as well as a reviewing competition, and the week can move towards a climax involving an evening when all the reviews are on display. Parents and pupils can be invited to attend the evening, at which the author speaks and presents the prizes. You can ensure a good-sized audience by not announcing the names of the prizewinners beforehand.

Whether or not a school's reading policy succeeds will depend ultimately on the drive and enthusiasm of the staff. To develop and extend teenagers' reading we must provide not only time and books, but a climate in which reading is seen to be a pleasurable and worthwhile activity.

14 The library service
Keith Stevens

The importance of the library within the secondary school has been well documented. For many, in fact most pupils, it is their *only* contact with books and reading materials which range from a daily newspaper to the latest popular thriller, or textbook required for academic work. Pupils who are not public library users, and who are not familiar with books in the home should have access to a wide range of attractive, up-to-date books and magazines to support their school work, to encourage and stimulate them to read for pleasure, and to enhance their hobbies and interests. The school library should, in the broadest sense, widen and enrich the lives of all its users, offering the chance to develop their experience of life, as well as simply to learn.

Secondary school libraries in the City of Newcastle are organized by the Education Library Service. In fact, the Education Library Service is the agency responsible for providing central library services to *all* the schools within the metropolitan district. The service is totally funded by Education, and covers the authority's 160 schools from nursery level up to secondary and high-school level. The secondary and high schools receive the full-time assistance of a library assistant, and the half-time assistance of a chartered librarian, (one chartered librarian is shared between two paired schools). The services to children through the public library service are separated from the Education Library Service, and are funded by a different committee, although formal and informal liaison takes place between the children's librarian and the education librarian.

Each individual secondary school and high school (in common with every school in the authority) receives a generous allowance for the purchase of school library stock every year. The level of this allowance is controlled by the factor of the number of children on roll at any one time, and therefore fluctuates as numbers on roll vary. The selection of stock for the secondary and high schools is normally totally under the control of the school librarian, although teachers usually suggest titles for addition to stock. But it is the librarian who has to take the overview in order to ensure a balanced stock between all age levels, abilities and subjects.

The Education Library Service operates from a central point in the central library, although the majority of the staff are employed to undertake work in the schools. The Education Library is permanently staffed, and is available for use both in term time and during the vacation by teachers living in, or working for, the City of Newcastle.

The Education Library comprises two main sections, which are physically divided into two rooms:

(a) Primary collection – comprising all books suitable for children up to the age of 11–12 years (both fiction and non-fiction, and a large collection of material suitable for project use and individualized learning, including a growing collection of non-print media).

(b) Secondary collection – containing all the resources for secondary and high school pupils.

It is this secondary collection on which we will dwell for the remainder of this chapter.

The secondary collection is well-balanced, and reflects all subjects, abilities and age levels. It is a policy of the Education Library Service to purchase a copy of every fiction book published to add to the collection. Normally, the majority of non-fiction published is also purchased although a number are rejected for a variety of reasons. In this way, the collection acts both as an exhibition collection, and as a loan stock service.

Demands are heaviest on the Education Library stock with regard to the very popular non-fiction which school librarians are unable to supply in enough quantity to satisfy demand. Examples which spring to mind here include books on motorcycles, war, horror, pop stars, film and television personalities, etc. – the perennial favourites. These popular non-fiction topics often provide the answer to the non-reading teenager – he may not read a work of fiction but he may well consult one of these.

Secondary school librarians tend to borrow only infrequently from the secondary fiction bookstock, largely because of the good

E

fiction coverage which most secondary schools enjoy (all secondary schools have in the region of 18,000–20,000 volumes). However, the stock is available at all times should the school librarian ever wish to consult it. The collection has been utilized recently for the following purposes: a teenage fiction display, a fantasy fiction display, a television inspired book display etc. School librarians have taken the opportunity to inject some new titles into their collections, and to replace delapidated stock.

On the whole, the greatest use made of the secondary collection is project-based, and the fiction element is less important. Nevertheless, the space devoted to the fiction collection is justified, and attempts are being made to extend the use made of the stock. Many more paperbacks are being purchased, particularly adult fiction, and the hardback stock is declining in proportion. This swing towards paperbacks has been occasioned by the teenagers' preference for their reading matter in this format. Many reasons have been put forward in order to ascertain the answer to this visible trend. Paramount among them would seem to be ease of use, colourful expressive jackets, and lastly, and probably most importantly, the fallacious belief that somehow the paperback is shorter.

At the other end of the scale, a sizeable proportion of the book-fund has been spent on 'special readers', 'easy readers', 'short reads', 'books that anyone can read', etc. (the search for a kinder term for 'remedial readers' goes on!)

Many able readers, who for one reason or another, will not tackle a full length novel will often be prepared to read a book from this category.

Teenagers do not visit the Education Library to choose their own books. The service is available to teachers and librarians, and as such we act as the 'middlemen' between the children and the books. In the school library, the concept of 'middlemen' also exists, with often much guidance being given to aid selection of suitable reading material for the individual.

The type of material borrowed from the secondary school libraries depends very much on the type of reader. The readers can be classified into five distinct groupings, which roughly coincide with their year-groups. They are:

(a) the mature sixth former

(b) the less academic sixth former

(c) the CSE candidates and fifth formers

(d) the problem area of the third and fourth formers

(e) the new intake, the 11–13 year olds.

The mature sixth former's school life revolves around academic work, and his interest is often in literature rather than fiction, particularly when English features as a subject for special examination attention. Boys rarely seem to read 'teenage' fiction, but seem to concentrate on 'adult' fiction, e.g. Frederick Forsyth, Alistair Maclean, Hammond Innes, Ian Fleming etc. Girls are attracted towards the more 'heavy' historical fiction – e.g. Anya Seton, Catherine Gaskin – and contemporary women's authors such as Margaret Drabble and Beryl Bainbridge. The more modern fiction, with a few exceptions such as Gunnel Beckman, Honor Arundel, Joan Lingard – they seem to ignore unless they are pushed.

Not surprisingly, the priorities for fiction with the less academic sixth former are somewhat different from the academic sixth former. Series take on a greater importance, with Topliners and Pyramids being read almost to the exclusion of all else. A great number of authors write particularly for the teenage reader market, and these authors are read by this less academic group. Of special note would be Gunnel Beckman again, K. M. Peyton (particularly the Pennington series), Joan Lingard, Roy Brown, John Rowe Townsend, Faroukh Dhondy, Christopher Leach, J. L. Foster's anthologies, Joan Tate, Paul Zindel, Charlotte Zolotow, Jill Chaney, etc. A good stock of this type of fiction will generally encourage the older teenager to read. I am against separating the 'teenage' collection in the school library and would prefer it totally integrated with the 'adult stock' – the main reason being that teenagers dislike being categorized, and a completely separated bookstock reinforces this categorization. If the stock is intershelved with the adult stock the teenager can easily make the transition from 'teenread' to adult novel. I prefer to see merely a division of stock into two: what might be called 'junior fiction' (11–13), and 'senior fiction', containing books suitable for 14 plus.

The CSE examination groups provide a third distinct group regarding the type of reader. Fifth-form girls need much encouragement and guidance as they tend to consider there is nothing that will relate and appeal to them. Of course there are many books on the theme of teenagers and their relationships, but the librarian must be prepared to be told that the books are patronizing, or 'not real', or childish. Books which the librarian may feel would be interesting to the teenager, particularly the boys, are often rejected by the readers. A generous popular non-fiction supply is essential if the older boys are to use the library at all, particularly books on popular sports.

Particularly reluctant readers may be encouraged by the use of a collection of fiction for use within the English department on teenage themes, although preparation and annotation are required beforehand. For example, some of the differences between Gunnel Beckman's *Mia* and Inge Krog's *Fourteen Days Overdue* could be suggested, and the pupils asked to comment further on the novels.

Many social and environmental problems are covered by this category of fiction; John Branfield's *Nancekuke* concerns nuclear energy, while John Rowe Townsend's *Noah's Castle* envisages a future of economic disaster. Books dealing with the future could possibly be compared to Ray Bradbury and the popular science fiction writers. Joan Lingard's Irish-inspired series about a Protestant and Catholic couple in Northern Ireland should arouse comment and discussion amongst both the boys and the girls. Almost all the other usual topics, namely drugs, sex, friendships, illnesses both physical and mental, relationships between parents and children, teachers and pupils, marriage, work, and racial harmony and tension, are more than adequately covered by the all-embracing term 'teenage fiction'.

At the librarian's discretion, it may be useful to purchase very light fiction, almost certainly in paperback, for the reluctant reader. Light romances such as Mills and Boon, westerns, war stories – the staple diet of many public library users – may fill the gap, and at least provide an answer to the pupil who will not read anything.

The final two categories of type of reader will be dealt with together. These categories cover the children in the age ranges 11–13, and 13–14 years. A wide selection of popular children's authors and fiction must be part of the secondary school library. This is to enable first-year pupils to continue their reading and interest in authors and to offer another chance to the pupils who may not have been introduced to a wide range of children's literature, and who are not members of their local library. Authors in this category might include: Joan Aiken (some of her titles), Michael Bond, C. S. Lewis, Susan Cooper, Roald Dahl, Alan Garner etc.

Another category of fiction which is essential to any secondary school library are the film and television spin-offs. At the age when pupils tend to give up using the library, around 14–15 years of age, they can sometimes be attracted to read books about their favourite television or film characters. Examples here would be *Dr Who*, *The Good Life, Star Wars, Jaws* etc.

With limited resources, the school librarian has the difficult decision to make between buying fiction which may not be especially well read, and buying some non-fiction which will almost certainly be used until it falls apart. Paperbacks make it possible to build up a fiction collection with limited resources, although it is sometimes difficult to obtain all the titles one would wish in paperback format.

Constant displays of fiction certainly encourage use, sometimes to the extent of having to keep reserve copies of the popular titles, and series such as Topliners will often have to be provided in at least duplicate. Reviewing magazines, posters, competitions, etc. can all be successfully used to encourage reading, although the older teenager is generally reluctant to discuss his personal reading, particularly with regard to fiction. Often the only guideline for the librarian is the number of times that particular titles have been issued, but this alone can be at the same time, encouraging and misleading.

Book selection for any particular group of readers does not radically differ from selection for another group. Accordingly teenage book selection follows the same pattern as primary school book selection. One area for concern with teenage book selection is the question of series. Two good examples are the Peacock and the Topliner series: in both cases, there are some titles which may give cause for concern, and each title has to be assessed on its own merits. Nevertheless, on the whole, the series are very good value for this age group. Book selection is undertaken using the following aids:

(a) approval service – the Education Library Service receives an approval service from a recognized library supplier (as most school library services do). This is the main route whereby most new titles enter stock. As many titles as possible are thoroughly reviewed, although all are assessed. All teachers and librarians have access to these new books, and the titles can be handled, assessed, rejected or selected for addition to stock. Due to the nature of some titles available for teenagers, it is considered desirable that all books for teenagers are assessed for suitability for inclusion in the school library. Books which do slip through the 'net' are retrieved later when the title is brought to our attention, or a complaint is received. The title is then read by the Education Librarian, and a decision made as to whether the book should be removed from the open shelves. This occurs infrequently, the last recorded instance concerned Judy Blume's *Forever* which is still available in the school libraries, although on application to the school librarian, at her discretion.

(b) library supplier slips – approval slips from the leading library suppliers are also consulted and perused. In this way, it is hoped that a blanket coverage is achieved. Purchasing books without handling them has obvious disadvantages, and this form of purchase is used only sparingly.

(c) review journals – a comprehensive range of reviewing journals are subscribed to, and these are used to fill in any gaps in stock which have not been covered by the approval service or the approval slips. Of particular value are the annotated lists compiled by the Youth Libraries Group of the Library Association and the School Librarian.

(d) local reviewing journals – the Education Library Service operate a *Readers' Review Panel Magazine* in which librarians, teachers, teacher/librarians, library school students and pupils all cooperate to review new additions to the Education Library. Many reviews are submitted for inclusion by teenagers and for teenagers. A magazine containing all the reviews is published three times a year.

(e) bulk buys – regular visits are made to a library supplier for bulk additions to stock.

After purchase, regular displays of new titles added to stock are mounted in the libraries concerned.

What should the relationships be between the library and the classroom? When children enter a secondary school for the first time they generally receive a timetabled library period for the first two years or so, up to the age of around fourteen years. After that it is assumed that the reading habit has been instilled and due to demands made by the examination syllabus, the library lesson often disappears from the timetable. This is to be regretted because this is the very time when many children seem to drift away from reading and visiting libraries. It is expected that children will make their own way to the school library or public library, but many do not. The library needs to be dynamic, active, and fully aware of the potential which it possesses in order to capture these lapsed readers, and reintroduce them to the value of reading as quickly as possible.

Links with the classroom should not end here of course. So far, or until very recently, it has largely been assumed that the library is closely related to, and therefore should come under the wing of, the English department but, increasingly, the library must be seen as a unifying force within the school linking all subjects across the curriculum. Teenagers, especially, could be encouraged to link their academic work with relevant fiction – the use of fiction in subject areas other than English should not be neglected. How valid many of the books by Ronald Welch, the Trease and Treece writers, Mollie Hunter, and Rosemary Sutcliffe could be to the History department. What about Ben Bova in relation to Geography, and so on – the list is endless. For too long the library has been seen as the extension of the English department and it is time that this stronghold be broken. This requires the staff, who traditionally do not relate to the library, to be shown the benefits and value of the library and they must be convinced of the educational value of the resource. Only if they are convinced of this will they promote the use of the library to their pupils. Is this one of the reasons why teenage use of the library drops off? Perhaps they are not receiving enough encouragement from their own teachers in the classroom.

The other important link concerns the position of the library *vis-a-vis* the home. In the past it was naively assumed that the child in the school was the sole user of the library. Increasingly, the child is being seen as the 'go-between' between the school library and the home. Books are being chosen on behalf of other members of the family, who would not visit the public library, or have access to its resources. The readership of the school library is often far in excess of the 1200 pupils and 80 staff, who would seem to be its immediate users. The advent of the dual purpose library and community school is particularly important in this context.

Through some of the literature written specifically for them, teenagers are able to solve some of the problems facing them at home and hence foster an improved link between the home and the school. They are able to cope with and to understand many of the problems and anxieties facing them during adolescence by reading about them. The problems of the home, growing up, conflict with parents etc. are all covered in teenage books, and the books help to bridge the gap between the individual and the school, the individual and the home, and hence the home and the school.

One of the basic aims of the school librarian must be to foster familiarity with, and enjoyment of, the school library. The library must be a vital part of the school's life and reflect the aims, objectives and goals of the school. It is required to be a support service to all pupils and staff and therefore cannot operate in isolation from the rest of the school. The school library must be a part of the community and serve it, but the community must be educated to use the library properly and develop it, as well as the readers themselves, to their full potential.

More emphasis should be placed on audiovisual materials as undoubtedly the pupils are familiar with this type of material, and the equipment necessary to exploit it. The library must keep abreast of all new developments, not only in its information resources, but also in its methods of dissemination. The possibility of exploitation of new media to recapture 'lost' readers amongst teenagers needs to be fully investigated. One plausible reason for their lack of interest in reading is the obvious correlation with an increase in television viewing. We should use this fact to attempt to attract them back to the reading habit.

The range of material specifically written for teenagers has widened, been improved, and made more attractive than ever before. No longer is it necessary to 'steal' books from the adult library, the teenager now has an adequate supply of his own. It is now up to the school library, the librarian and the teachers to exploit the material available.

15 The library and the curriculum
Cecilia Gordon

The objectives and purpose, in fact the whole *raison d'être* of a school library, have never been better defined than they were in a DES pamphlet published in 1967.[1] In those days the library was only a book room but the principles remain the same today and the educational ideal should be the credo of every school librarian, not least those who have achieved a multi-media resource centre in which reading books is a way of using a specially designed medium and all media are classified and catalogued uniformly according to subject content.

The essence of this Pamphlet No 21 was deftly summarized in a later DES publication in 1973:[2]

> It is the function of the school library to be the centre of the intellectual life of the school, available at all times for reference, study and private reading; it should support the teaching of the subjects of the curriculum by providing books for reference, for background reading and for further study and a place where they can conveniently be studied; but it has a specific purpose beyond its relations to subjects namely *to make readers* – and in this fact and fiction, reference and recreation all have their part to play.

In 1979 consider how many of those admirable ideals are now in danger of neglect and are, in fact, highly vulnerable. Educational provision varies disastrously from Local Education Authority to Local Education Authority. Education is politically manipulated and the provision of library services to schools and of staff, stock and accommodation within schools have been, in many cases, the chosen victims of swingeing financial cuts. To add to the problems each individual school has to resolve, in order to provide a library service suited to its resources (financial and staff) there have been enormous changes in curriculum ideas in secondary schools, especially since the advent of CSE.

There are as yet no *generally* accepted standards for staffing school libraries in the UK in spite of firm recommendations from the School Library Association,[3] the Library Association[4] and, more recently, the Centre for Educational Technology[5] – not to mention numerous books and articles in the professional press. Clearly defined roles of personnel involved in running a library resource centre, as well as inservice training of both teachers and pupils, are essential if the library is to provide adequate support to the curriculum.

To avoid tactful circumlocution or vague terminology, thus bypassing arguments about suitable qualifications and titles I shall describe the person in charge of the library as 'the librarian'. However little time such a person has to devote to the library, whatever her qualifications may be, it can be safely assumed that one person will be regarded as being in charge of routine and organization and will order stock in collaboration and agreement with others.

I would like first to consider the 'winds of change' that have, during the last two decades, blown through many a school library scattering carefully planned stock and confusing the image of the library for both teachers and pupils.

It is not the librarian's job to suggest curriculum innovation but it is essential that the library should be an educational tool to support the chosen curriculum and that the encouragement of recreational reading should not be forgotten. Fiction should not be regarded as the sole source of recreational reading. I have heard pupils (especially boys) called 'non-readers' when in fact, a little investigation revealed that they were actually avid readers. They read about things that interested them, but rejected stories. Of course there is no denying the value of reading imaginative books, not to do so is to miss one of the most enriching experiences of life. But such a pupil as I have mentioned is unjustly described as a 'non-reader'.

Supporting the curriculum cannot be done unless there is proper communication between the librarian and the rest of the staff and also a good 'early warning' system so that the right materials can be available at the right time. All librarians should be obliged to attend staff meetings and should try, as far as possible, to take part in curriculum discussions.

At the moment, however, anyone visiting schools around the

country, and also reading educational magazines would find it hard not to conclude that British secondary education is in a state of flux and change, sometimes even panic! This inevitably affects the library provision within the school and the support services from without. Local Education Authorities appear to have so many and varied expectations of school libraries and even schools under the same authority can differ widely in their attitudes. Tactful investigation often reveals that the estimate of the library's importance is that of the head teacher. This is not of course always true. Deep disagreements among the staff can make it difficult for the library to provide a useful, consistent service.

It is fair to assume that most secondary schools are now using audiovisual media both for teaching and learning and one hopes any catalogues or lists will include all media. To a librarian, the only new problems posed by non-book materials are those of storage and security. These require separate consideration from book care.

Recently the SLA published a most helpful booklet *Non-book media in Junior Schools: a handbook of practical advice* by Peter James.[6] This can also be commended to secondary schools because it deals with a specific problem relating to non-book media. Audiovisual material comes in all sorts of shapes and sizes and, although it can be classified by its subject matter as easily as books are, it is not as easily stored. Books go on shelves of standard sizes and these will accommodate only some audiovisual materials. Some librarians in schools and some in teachers' centres have attempted multi-media storage as well as multi-media cataloguing. But this is not an un-qualified success and most schools shelve or store non-book materials by medium in subject order. Peter James deals with the individual problems of each medium and gives sensible practical advice on accommodating and caring for things as diverse as shells and charts!

While it cannot be denied that the vital ingredient of any learning/teaching material is its subject matter it must also be admitted that some teachers prefer to use one medium rather than another and some pupils find it easier to learn by listening and others by looking. Some even prefer to read!

As the Bullock report said:[7]

We cannot accept that the printed word should learn to adjust to a modified status. In analysing the reading process we argued that the medium of print occupies, and will continue to occupy, a position of the highest importance in the educational process.

So, separating media can be more than just a matter of convenience.

In 1962 when I took over the library in a large ILEA mixed comprehensive school the link with the curriculum and the library stock was firmly subject-based. The idea of what constituted a relevant stock of information books was in many ways very different from today. In many schools the same attitude still prevails and is often rather snidely referred to as 'in the grammar school tradition'. To help me with my choice of stock I regularly circulated heads of departments, and teachers whom I knew to be interested in the library, and reminded them that a book order would be going in during the half-term break, or the school holidays, and that I would be grateful for suggestions for suitable additions to the school library. This soon became unnecessary because after a term or two teachers would bring me, at all seasons, cuttings or short book lists. I reserved the right to decide what should be bought, maintaining that I had an overall knowledge of the stock. Also, in those days, the distinction between a textbook (which should be bought for use in lessons) and a library book was fairly clear. Now the difference is less obvious. I seldom bought more than two copies of an information book. 'Sets are for classrooms', I said. All the time I kept a wary eye open for subject gaps. If I failed to answer a query I tried to remedy this by finding and buying a book to fill the need. The reference section was small and conventional: dictionaries in several languages, books of quotations etc. In fact, what is often referred to in public libraries as 'the quick reference section', backed up of course by several sets of encyclopedias suited to various ages and abilities.

First-year pupils had a carefully planned course of library instruction and some teaching in the use and care of reference and information books. This instruction was given by me to small groups extracted from the classes who came on regular weekly visits. The teacher controlled pupils who were browsing, reading or choosing books for home loans. Thus I worked through each class until every pupil had had a session with me. Fiction reading was not neglected; we would sometimes spend time discussing books pupils had returned which led to recommendations from pupils (very useful and often very revealing!) and suggestions from me. Higher up in the school teachers would book occasional periods for classes to come to the library 'to encourage their reading' and some-times to do subject based research.

Then came CSE and particularly CSE Mode III. Pupils were now doing individual research and needed books such as I would pre-viously have expected to find in a classroom. Several pupils would be doing related projects or even pursuing the same lines of research. Many books were obviously useful for several subject areas. So I began, unwillingly, to buy multiple copies (perhaps even as many as six!) and to take a good hard look at my reference section. The demands made on the library by GCE and O level candidates were of course still subject-based, as were those by the third-year pupils.

CSE brought back to the library pupils who had never crossed the threshold since their first year. Most of them seemed pleased to be there and many took the opportunity to borrow books of their own choice for home reading.

However, their projects varied considerably both in content and quality. Few pupils had any idea how to scan, had forgotten how to use an index, and were quite incapable of making notes or rewriting material in their own words. Things seem no better today.

'Libraries and Project Work' in SLA Members' *Newsletter* 21: 7 is a report resulting from an appeal made by a sub-committee of the SLA. Many valid points are made in what is a short summary of replies received. I will mention a few relevant to this article. Some people advocated broad topics (e.g. The Sea) from which in-dividuals could choose segments, thus spreading the pressure of demand on available material. It was regarded as essential to check in advance the material available, bearing in mind the age and ability of the pupils concerned. The librarian should be given adequate warning in case there was a need to obtain extra material. No men-tion is made in this report of the use of audiovisual material. The report comments on the skills needed to produce a good project, skimming, skipping, using indexes etc. as well as finding the right books. It should not *still* be necessary to reiterate this.

Reading for specific information is quite a different skill from reading narrative. One correspondent remarked 'If teachers would set themselves a project – even the outline of one – they would begin to realize what they are expecting from their pupils.' Michael

Marland once said, and I quote from memory, 'We ask a person to find out all they can about a chosen subject, to make notes and abstracts, rewrite their discoveries in their own words, make a contents list, produce illustrations and an index. At primary school this is called a topic, at secondary a project and at University a Ph.D.' Reading for information needs to be specifically taught; teachers constantly complain about the standard of CSE project work but it is unusual to find any formal instruction for pupils on how to do a project.

To return to the pattern of change. The advent of ROSLA brought a whole new set of problems and attitudes into the library. Most teachers seemed ill-prepared when finally confronted by a situation they had been forewarned about. Desperate attempts were made to devise courses to interest pupils who were furious at being kept on at school. Their older siblings had been allowed to leave at fourteen and were now making money 'on the barrows' or in Marks and Spencers. Attendances were irregular and the general attitude often mutinous. The situation calmed down after a couple of years but I blame ROSLA for the increased use of worksheets which, as a librarian, I deplore. Of course I know why people photocopy relevant sections out of books and pass the sheets round the class. One book will service a whole class and money is saved while the copyright law continues to be broken. But this is not teaching pupils how to find information, it is simply making them accept what the teacher wants them to learn and the library makes a very small contribution to this method.

Workcards do involve the library, consisting as they do of a set of questions, either on a particular subject or based on a particular book. However, many pupils simply regard completing a workcard as a kind of quiz game, a task to be completed as fast as possible. One wonders how much they learn and retain and how many are actually hostile to this method. Witness the little boy I met at the Pompeii exhibition. He was sitting sadly on the edge of a pseudo fountain. 'You don't look very happy,' I said. 'I'm not,' he replied. 'I came to see Pompeii and look what I've got – a bloody workcard!'

Could the comment, so often made about intelligence tests, be revised to apply to workcards 'All they prove is that you can fill in a workcard?' Far too few teachers who devise their own workcards realize that a question must be carefully phrased if it is to produce the right answer. Young people often think laterally. Donald Barnes warned of the danger of badly produced workcards and called the pupils' work 'industrious futility'.[8] It is treasure hunting, not education.

I have dwelt on workcards at such length because I do not think that they stimulate the proper use of the library or make it appear a source of pleasure and of information that a person will turn to all his life.

Just recently another blast of wind has gone through some secondary schools. They now teach a very wide curriculum of overall studies with a detailed syllabus for each branch of study chosen. This method is used with lower school pupils and is a post-primary school pattern. The programme will be called something like 'Humanities', 'Core studies', 'Mankind' or 'Integrated studies'. A humanities course will include English, Geography, History and Religious Education; groups of pupils will concentrate on different aspects until a wide area has been covered in two years. 'Creation', for instance, will include myths from all religions. Penelope Farmer's book on creation myths of the world is divided into sections which give some idea of how such a subject can be sub-divided: Earth, Man, Fire, Food plants, Death, The End and the Beginning.[9]

In practice this integrated studies method of teaching can mean that each class has twelve lessons a week with the same teacher, who may be any kind of subject teacher but is expected to cover all the ground previously planned. Good teachers use such a programme to teach library skills in collaboration with the librarian. Bad teachers can barely keep pace with the syllabus. This method of integrated teaching can be excellent with mixed-ability groups. The less able can choose some simple aspect of, let us say, 'The Romans', their houses or their food for instance, whilst brighter pupils concentrate in considerable detail on something more abstract which interests them. But as a librarian, I think these programmes are bad for the image of the library. Increasingly the classes are coming there only to do work set by the teacher or to complete workcards. More writing is done and less reading until the library becomes just like another classroom. A pupil should see the purposeful use of the library as something different from 'lessons' and so be less likely to see it as a 'school thing' he will discard when he leaves.

Opportunities to browse and make a free choice of a book to

read for pleasure become fewer. Lunch times and after school hours are sometimes the only opportunities left and at these times discipline can be the main problem and pupil and librarian have little chance of personal contact and discussion.

Now consider this learning programme, described in only very general terms, from the point of view of managing the library resource centre, choosing stock and giving real support to the curriculum. At any point in time there may be 250 children 'doing' the Romans. The librarian is thus forced to buy sets of books, which is not only expensive but can seriously unbalance the stock. Certain books may be strongly recommended; but what are the criteria for a really good book to use with projects? We do not want to give the pupils a 'package deal' and be back to where we started with the danger of 'mindless copying'. One solution to the problem of so many pupils doing similar projects is to 'freeze' a large part of the stock, refuse to let it go out on loan and so ensure that books required are never out. Depending on numerous sets of encyclopedias is another solution but this is not a very inspired way of learning. Schools which are trying to maintain the service and support one would like a library to give, and also help with a wide curriculum, sometimes have mini-resource centres for each year, to support the library. But these grow until they are much larger than classroom collections and need someone, other than the librarian, to organize, administer and check them. They should be linked by uniform cataloguing and classifying to the library stock and ultimately a union catalogue should be built up showing what is available in the whole school to encourage teachers to share materials.

Another solution is to have the library resource centre used *solely* for reference and research. Classes, or large groups come there to do individual work and all the first years have a timetabled induction course and are issued with a handout on the organization of the resource centre. They also take part in a 'resource hunt', based on a workcard dealing with a particular subject and linking all resources. After this they are expected to learn how to work through a project using various media.

There should be staff induction courses for all new members of staff and sixth-form pupils need refresher courses in library skills before they leave school. These should include learning how to use advanced, complicated reference books like Keesing's *Contemporary Archives*. But such courses are not easy to arrange as sixth-form pupils tend to 'vanish' after they have completed their A levels.

Another useful way of using such a resource centre is to have a printed booking form for arranging visits for small groups scheduled to come at times when the centre is free. A teacher makes the booking and the pupils come with this form, which includes a list of their names and the purpose of their visit. The librarian looks after these pupils without help from the teacher.

In addition to the main resource centre, one school has three satellite resource rooms on three separate floors, each floor consisting of classrooms devoted to one subject area. Eventually it is hoped to catalogue the material in these rooms, mostly non-book print material, but with some audiovisual hard and software including references in the main catalogue.

A school which has the arrangements described above also has an entirely separate lending library for home loans. Here are found information books, suitable for homework or individual interests, and fiction, mostly in paperback. There are staffing problems (of course). The resource centre is available all day and in the charge of the librarian (who is full time and qualified) but the lending library, when open, is in the charge of a clerical assistant who works only twenty-five hours a week, so its availability is more limited.

I mentioned sixth-form refresher courses but a much more pressing problem is that of providing proper facilities for sixth-form private study. In many schools there is an area in the library reserved for sixth-form study provided with reference books suitable for their level of study. But it is difficult to provide enough privacy and silence anywhere near the working area of the average library with its constant comings and goings. Other schools do manage to provide a separate room for private study but, adolescents being what they are, this is very liable to become a kind of club room unless a teacher is responsible for seeing that it is properly used.

In various parts of the country, sixth-form colleges are now being built as separate establishments and in other areas neighbourhood schools are combining their sixth forms to provide viable teaching units with a reasonable teacher-pupil ratio. In some cases pupils visit each other's schools. In others, particularly where there are two single sex schools close together, it has been possible to build a 'sixth form block' shared by both schools. There are problems here regarding the selection of material. Is it possible to provide an adequate sixth-form library in addition to those in the two schools?

To sum up, and underline points already made, I think it is necessary to say categorically that no matter how well chosen and professionally arranged a library resource centre may be, it can still be grossly under used and under appreciated. Materials must be freely available and this implies adequate staffing, furthermore, unless teachers and pupils have received adequate training in information retrieval and the full exploitation of materials available, their educational value is reduced.

As previously stated, the inadequate staffing of most secondary school libraries is a cause for grave concern and the ill considered economies made by reducing the numbers of ancillary/clerical helpers has made matters worse. I mentioned earlier that the SLA and the LA have both published authoritative statements on staffing. Complaints appear again and again in the professional press but one still finds library resource centres run by inadequately qualified people who are given ludicrously little time to do the job. The Council for Educational Technology is devising a proper staff structure for support staff. Its initial investigations revealed a state of confusion which surprised no one! As the result of a great deal of hard work and consultation, in which the Library Association was also involved, the Council issued a document 'An Outline Structure for Support Staff in Educational Technology'.[10] This consists mainly of a diagram but represents a great deal of investigation and discussion. It goes in detail into the nomenclature, training requirements and demands of each job. A second report is in hand now which contains a hierarchy of skills and is intended for use by anyone concerned in developing training courses for support staff. The word 'hierarchy' is very important. A library needs a director of studies who has an overall knowledge of the curriculum and its links with library use; but it also needs the expertise and reorganizational skills of a fully trained librarian, or dually qualified teacher/librarian. This person should rank as a head of department and carry authority.

Teacher training in the use of the library is too often woefully inadequate. The fact that I had to mention earlier 'induction courses' for new teachers is indicative of this and was said because over and over again comments are made about teachers not being taught to use modern library resource centres.

Several colleges have told me that they are putting on special courses in study skills for new students. This of course shows that the students have not received adequate training in their schools *but* it also suggests that some advanced training in library skills should be included in the syllabus of every College of Education.

Pupils arrive at their secondary schools with varied ideas about how to use a library resource centre. How much they already know about library organization and information retrieval is conditioned by the attitudes (educational and practical) that they have left behind them. This is more a matter of primary school methods than of merit. Some primary schools have a central library properly classified and catalogued, plus small reference collections in classrooms. Others have large collections in classrooms which are changed at intervals (termly perhaps) from some central stock which may or may not be available to pupils or staff to answer some query or supply a need. Others receive large loans from the Schools Library Service, for varying lengths of time. Many open plan schools have no central library but have subject areas from which material can be borrowed. Children in this type of school are able to move around freely and find what they want and the classification system is usually broad, so they learn to browse and choose. Sad to say, some primary schools cannot be said to have a library at all, only classroom collections which can remain in one classroom long after the children have lost interest in them.

Some pupils arrive with an unfortunate idea that there are 'reading books' and 'library' books. Many seem to have learnt to read without acquiring real understanding and enjoyment. So for many, there is a distinction between the books they are told to read and the ones they choose to read for themselves.

The majority of secondary schools do try to give their first-year pupils a structured course in library use. It is safe to assume that some will know next to nothing, others will have forgotten and yet others will be totally bewildered. Those who are already well informed can give valuable help in guiding others.

Growing concern about pupils' inability to use libraries productively led to the setting up of a British Library Research and Development Project, based at Liverpool Polytechnic from 1977 to 1978.

The hard work was done by Ann Irving who interviewed teachers and librarians in a selection of schools in Cheshire and Nottinghamshire and who also directly observed library instruction sessions. Her comments and findings are admirably summed up in *Education Libraries Bulletin* Vol. 21 part 2 published by the University of London.[11] No one was really surprised at what she found except Auriol Stevens in the *Observer* who seemed rather appalled that children are not being taught how to use books and libraries. She did however comment that 'Learning to find information and make clear notes are essential skills for academic success'. This pinpoints an aspect of pupil training which does need immediate attention. Very few pupils are taught how to make notes, as the SLA research found out.

Giving a sad backward glance at those ideals I began with I wonder now whether it is possible to live up to them. Were we attempting too much in those days, trying to cover too much ground, trying to encourage reading for pleasure and also provide an educational tool, trying to instil a love of reading as well as an ability to do personal research and find everyday information? Perhaps the time has come when we should regard the school library as purely an information retrieval centre and rely on the school bookshop, the public library and a few interested English teachers to encourage the reading of fiction? Maybe that is the answer and is the kind of support the curriculum demands. The early public libraries were loth to buy fiction but I can't help feeling it would be a tragedy to follow their example and run the risk of denying pupils from bookless homes access to fiction. Classroom collections, regularly changed, following the pattern of many primary schools, might be one answer. But the *average* secondary classroom could not accommodate an adequate collection, even if it were only paperbacks.

Alternatively, should the library be prepared to supply multi-media subject-based collections to be used by specific groups outside the library? But who could afford to do this? It would involve either duplicate buying or denying (maybe for a whole term) large 'chunks' of stock to pupils visiting the library. It is comforting to know that concern for school libraries is worldwide. The Library Association reported in the Library Association Record of February 1979 that the International Federation of Library Associations had drawn up the following draft resolution:

Whereas information is considered a national resource and access to it a basic right, and whereas each country develops its own national plan for library and information systems, and whereas school libraries provide access to information for the school and its community, be it resolved that school libraries be included and supported in all national planning for the provision of library and information services.[12]

As a final postscript it must be admitted that no school library resource centre can function unsupported by outside services. These can never replace individuals on the spot; but they can, and do, provide invaluable back-up advice and material to meet many needs. The pity is that the dissemination of information of what is locally (and nationally) available is often so poor. Many schools are totally unaware of what is available on their doorsteps. They may, for instance, spend money on expensive reprographic equipment when the copying could be done for them at a nearby teachers' centre.

It is not unreasonable for a school to expect to be able to call upon the majority of the following services to help them. The thing to hope for is a really supportive local schools' library service, from this you may often obtain a standard subject index, bulk loans on specific subjects, or topic boxes containing multi-media materials. The materials will be chosen as suitable for the age and ability of the pupils you specify. There should be a permanent exhibition of 'in print' books to help you choose stock, some places have software and equipment exhibited too. In rural areas, vans tour schools and teachers can make a choice from them. Most areas have advisors who will visit schools and discuss problems. Exeter and London both have regional resource centres where teachers can study software and learn to use it with compatible equipment – there must be other centres in different parts of the country. Teachers' centres should have displays too, some have mini-resource centres set up to show what can be done, some loan media. Nearly all can make slides and do printing and photocopying and all run in-service courses, most of which include one on library organization, book selection and cataloguing. Nearly all museums are helpful to schools. They will often lend artifacts and are always helpful to visiting school parties. A school's degree of involvement with the public library depends on the local government situation – a question of who pays for what.

But most public libraries will help schools as much as they can. Children should be encouraged to use the public library and it is a good idea to keep a stock of 'joining forms' in the school. In return, a school librarian can often help a public librarian to recover overdue books by making direct contact with a defaulter! Local history societies are invaluable sources of information. Some print local reminiscences and have copies of old photos and documents. These may be for sale or the society may be willing to let you have photocopies of them and also of old documents. All school librarians should be members of the School Library Association. The local branch will hold regular meetings with visiting speakers, exhibitions, discussions and seminars. It is possible to obtain a great deal of free material for school work. The *Times Education Supplement* used to advertise these, or point them out in short critical paragraphs. Now the best source of information is a book *Treasure Chest for Teachers*.[13] No school should be without a copy!

Notes

1 *The School Library*. Department of Education and Science Education Pamphlet Number 21. HMSO 1967
2 The Public Library Source: reorganisation and after. DES Library Information Series No. 2. HMSO 1973
3 *The Staffing of Secondary School Libraries*. School Library Association 1970
4 *Library Resource Provision in Schools: guidelines and recommendations*. Library Association 1977
5 See note 10
6 *Non-book media in Junior Schools: a handbook of practical advice*, Peter James. School Library Association 1977
7 DES *Language for Life: the Bullock Report*. Ch. 21: 1 1975
8 *From Communication to Curriculum*. Donald Barnes, Penguin 1975
9 *Beginnings: creation myths of the world, compiled and edited by Penelope Farmer*. Chatto & Windus
10 *Librarians need proper support as educational methods change*, Norman Willis. (Assistant Director CET) Library Association Record December 1978 Vol 80 (12)
11 Education Libraries' Bulletin. Summer 1978 Vol. 21 part 2 (Whole number 62) Institute of Education Library, University of London
12 Library Association Record Vol. 81 (2). This number also includes a report on IFLA: its effects and activities
13 *Treasure Chest for Teachers: services available to teachers and schools*. The Schoolmaster Publishing Co. Ltd

16   Sir, where can I get it?

Peter Kennerley

'Sir, where can I get it?' might well prove to be the most important question ever asked of me by one of my pupils. The question came at the end of a library lesson which I had been using to whet the appetite of my first-year secondary school boys for two novels. I had read an extract from one novel sufficiently well for one boy to wish to read the book for himself, but at that moment the library could not answer his need. There was nothing unique about my experience: any effective teacher presenting books with sensitivity and vigour is meeting the same problem; that of a number of children who want to read the book for themselves and faced with the long wait as their name rises slowly to the top of the library book request list. By the end of a month, that initial enthusiasm may well have melted away.

No librarian of my acquaintance can produce to order multiple copies of any book which, for whatever reason, achieves sudden popularity, and any teacher or librarian met by an interest in and demand for a book, knows that he is doing only half his job unless he can make that book easily available to the pupils.

My reply to 'Sir, where can I get it?' was to start what seems to have been the first school bookshop in the country, and the responses of a wide range of pupils and staff in that school were dramatic. People who were not in the habit of going into a bookshop, people who had not hitherto been the owners of many books, started to buy paperbacks for themselves because they wanted to.

The voluntary nature of the school bookshop enterprise has always been important. At school, even in areas of inadequate provision, children are bombarded with books – text books, books to do with exercises and work, and for many children books have never been associated with pleasure. Lord Boyle, a former Minister of Education, highlighted this matter a long time ago:

The gap between books as alien objects and bookshops as alien places, and the recognition that books give the power to explore vast areas of experience, and a bookshop as an exciting storehouse, is simply enormous, but I am convinced that by providing books on the children's ground, by being prepared to listen to what they say when using it and what they ask, and by showing it to parents occasionally, we could be unleashing a new force in education . . .

Too many children, for a host of reasons, have been turned off books completely by the middle or early teenage years. The school bookshop is not going to solve all educational ills, but there is now ample evidence that it can help to counteract some of the problems. Sir Alec Clegg's view cannot be ignored:

> In my view this school bookshop movement may do more for children's reading than all the testing, examining and pedagogical tricks that have ever been devised. Indeed it may go far to reduce the reluctance to read which poor teaching and too much testing can bring about.

That book ownership was not only desirable but absolutely essential in the creation of the reader had been suspected from the evidence of their own experience by many teachers and librarians, but the publication of *Children and Their Books* in 1977 produced the statistical evidence, and followed this up with strong support for the school bookshop movement:

> Our data show a marked association between book ownership and amount of reading, and it seems clear that the possession of books can play an important role in fostering commitment to reading.

The Bullock Report, *A Language for Life*, published two years earlier had been unequivocal in its support, going so far as to say that it is 'The responsibility of the school to make it possible for children and parents together to see and select books which can be bought and taken home'.

None of this could have happened before the paperback revolution brought attractive books at modest prices before people who had never before owned books. These books did not look part of the apparatus of education. Their sale was not part of the timetabled regime of the school. The customer could visit the school bookshop when *he* wished to, and buy books which *he* wanted for himself. In many instances his choices were not great literature – so what? For too long we have been flinging 'the best of English literature' at our children whether they were ready for it or not, and this has caused half of our problems. The voluntary characteristic of the school bookshop cannot be stressed too highly. Some librarians have reported sorrowfully that many adolescent pupils never visit the library and borrow books, but some of these same reluctant borrowers are willing to spend their own money on books in the bookshop – provided that their needs are met by the stock. I am not suggesting that we peddle shelves full of soft porn, but that we do meet their real needs. I wonder how many school bookshops are stocking the novels of Judy Blume? They certainly ought to be.

At a time of economic restraint the presence of the school book-shop is doubly important. I am a total supporter of free lending libraries and free school textbooks, but I think we are doing our pupils a disservice if we do not encourage them to become book-owners, and help them by selling the books in school.

Freshness can be a characteristic of the bookshop stock in a way that it can never be of the library or textbook stock. Every month the bookshop ought to bring the new publications onto its shelves and into its display windows so that the customer will always know that there will be something new to see. The staff of the school must be made aware of new material, otherwise we have the wretched situation where the same book is read with the children at the same time every year, and the staff simply do not know what is happening in the book world. Teachers have a lot to do with their time, and if the bookshop brings a constant flow of good new material right into the school, the staff in general can have no excuse for not seeing and sampling new books. As teachers we must be thoroughly steeped in books, and *Children and Their Books* brings this home:

It is impossible to overstress the influence of the teacher's own knowledgeability about books. The right book brought forward at the right time can make all the difference to a child's reading development.

The actual physical process of bringing the right book to the right child has always been a problem with hardback editions. High prices ensure that the vast majority of hardback books for children are selected and purchased by adults: the children's book has to filter through the net of adult selection. The advent of the paperback and the school bookshop is starting to change this process – but only slowly and not completely. The teacher/bookseller may be exerting *too* strong an influence upon the nature of the stock. At least in the school bookshop, where the stock selection is broad-based, the child can browse amongst the stock and make his own purchase without adult intervention. As most children are not in the habit of visiting the average commercial bookshop, the opening of a school bookshop can be the dawn of a new era for children and their parents. When the children reach the teenage years, the situation becomes even more critical.

Any good commercial bookseller will have a children's department, or at least a few clearly identifiable racks or shelves so that a child customer knows where to go to find the books which might interest him. For the teenage customer the problems become acute. The last place he wishes to go to is a children's department, and the general adult stock leaves him totally at a loss. At a time of increasing independence and increasing financial resources this is disastrous. I have had at least one report of success where the bookseller has established a thriving teenage section in a children's department through the judicious mixing of adult and teenage material.

The good school bookshop in the secondary school can do a great deal to bring the right book and the right reader together because the stock can be carefully selected and displayed for the teenage reader, provided of course that the teacher running the shop is prepared to keep in touch with the speedily changing teenage culture and is uninhibited in the selection of stock. Misguided censorship will be damaging. For example, the young adult reader will inevitably be concerned about sexual issues. Any book selection policy which censors all books handling sexual matters is a denial of the idea that books can help the reader to understand himself and his environment. To refuse to stock works of high integrity just because of the subject matter is to drive the teenager towards the undercover reading of tawdry soft porn which may at least in the short term be damaging.

The school bookshop can make available a wide range of relevant books, uncluttered with silly academic exercises, as evidence that books can be exciting, relevant, amusing, disturbing, sensitive sources of pleasure. The school bookshop can begin to restore the fun principle which is so sadly and so frequently lacking in our school book policies.

Part Four
Guidelines

17 An A–Z of fiction for teenagers
Chris Kloet

About Adolescence

Much of the fiction written for and about today's teenagers gives the impression that the adolescent years are necessarily plagued by the four Ts – tension, trauma, turmoil and trouble. Surrounded as we are by hosts of novels dealing with hostility towards authority, parents and school, juvenile delinquency, maladjustment and identity crisis, as well as stories which explore topics such as sex and violence with a frankness which would have been unthinkable until recently, one could be forgiven for wondering where, in fiction, are the healthy, uncomplicated young people who make the transition from childhood to adulthood easily, naturally, and with the minimum amount of fuss or self-examination. Such young people are still around, mainly in the works of authors from an earlier writing era, such as Geoffrey Trease, Malcolm Saville and Elfrida Vipont. You'll also find them in DINOSAURS, so read on!

Addiction

Predictably, most teenage novels which explore the subject of drug-taking warn against the habit and portray the youthful addict as someone who has an inadequate personality. John Branfield's *The Scillies Trip* (Gollancz) is a fairly low-key account of a bored girl who uses pot-smoking as a means of escape from her suffocating home. Told from the viewpoint of her younger sister, the story explores sibling rivalry, as well as the destructive aspects of drug addiction. Similar themes are treated less successfully in Maria Rodman's *Tuned Out* (Topliner), a story about a boy's attempts to help his idolized elder brother kick the LSD habit. The moral dilemma faced by the boy who finds that his adoptive brother is a dope pusher is the theme of S. E. Hinton's *That Was Then, This Is Now* (Gollancz and Lions). This is a much better book because the characters are believable and the issue of drugs arises naturally from their harsh background. It's quite a tear-jerker and so too is the anonymous *Go Ask Alice* (Corgi). Based on the diary of a fifteen-year-old girl, this shows the stark realities of drug addiction with all the sordid details. A shocker in more ways than one, as some of the incidents and language could give offence. Anna Britton's *Fike's Point* (Angus and Robertson) set in Australia, is the story of a brother and sister and their drop-out culture parents who are overtaken by tragedy when the parents become addicts. For mature readers with strong stomachs. If they are perceptive they will also realize that the story touches on lesbianism.

Alcoholism is the topic of a few books for teenagers. Less able readers may enjoy Hans-Eric Hellberg's *Follow My Leader* (Topliner) in which the young protagonist sorts out his near-alcoholic dad, but it's all rather tame. A book which gives far greater insights into the causes and effects of alcoholism is Alison Prince's *The Doubting Kind* (Methuen, Topliner Redstar, two volumes). This is the story of one eventful week in the lives of two teenage girls, Fanny and Bobbie. Bobbie's father is involved in an accident and her alcoholic mother tries to deal with the crisis. A fast-moving, readable book which is admirably free from moralizing.

Adoption

One of the very best books on fostering and adoption is Rosa Guy's *Edith Jackson* (Gollancz) which describes a Black girl's efforts to keep her family of sisters together through a succession of awful foster homes. A sequel to *The Friends* (Gollancz and Puffin) this sombre story is suitable for mature readers. Several of the titles in the Topliner series explore other aspects of the subject, such as *Summer Girl* by Max Lundgren, in which a tough, delinquent girl is boarded out to holiday parents. There are some good, sensitive portraits here, particularly of the mentally retarded child of the family, but the character of the girl is not entirely credible. In *Sam and Me* by Joan Tate (Topliner) an adopted girl learns that if her marriage is to survive, she must become more than an emotional sponge. In *Answering Miss Roberts* by Christopher Leach (Topliner) an adopted girl's fantasies about her real mother land her in trouble. It seems a good place here to mention John Rowe Townsend's powerfully brooding novel of suspense *The Intruder* (OUP and Peacock) which has the question of a young man's true identity at its centre.

Adventure Stories

Many of the titles listed elsewhere under other headings could be called adventure stories of a type. Here, however, is a mini-list of authors not dealt with, by and large, elsewhere in the list, who write 'rattling good yarns' and provide a good, straightforward read, often for younger adolescents. Most of the authors have some titles available in paperback.

RICHARD ARMSTRONG: sea stories (Dent).

NINA BAWDEN: family adventures, younger readers (Gollancz and Puffin).

ROY BROWN: often stories about delinquent boys (Abelard Schuman and Puffin).

ARTHUR CATHERALL: sea, animal and war stories (Dent).

EILIS DILLON: sea and animal stories, set in Ireland (Faber and Puffin).

HELEN GRIFFITHS: animals (Hutchinson and Puffin).

JOHN HARRIS: First World War flying (Puffin).

DAVID LINE: murder plots and thugs (Cape and Puffin).

ALLAN CAMPBELL MCLEAN: historical adventures, Scottish Highlands (Collins and Lions).

J. M. MARKS: hi-jackings, jungle warfare (OUP and Puffin).

ALISON MORGAN: family adventures, Wales (Chatto and Puffin).

RICHARD PARKER: family adventure (Grasshopper and Puffin).

RICHARD PECK: Ghosts and kidnapping (Collins and Lions).

MALCOLM SAVILLE: family adventures and thrillers (Armada).

SYLVIA SHERRY: adventures, different locations (Cape and Puffin).

COLIN THIELE: land and sea adventures, Australia (Collins).

Aiken, Joan

Although her well-known fantastical melodramas of an 'imagined' nineteenth-century England, such as *The Cuckoo Tree* and *Midnight is a Place* (both Cape and Puffin) are popular with young adolescents, this author's other titles of special note to teenagers are *Go Saddle the Sea* (Cape), a picaresque novel about a young man's journey across Spain in the early nineteenth century; *A Bundle of Nerves* (Gollancz and Peacock), a collection of her spine-chilling short stories; *Night Fall* (Topliner) a convincing thriller.

Alternative Society

A witty book, which neither condemns nor condones the freaked-out alternative society is *I Never Loved Your Mind* by Paul Zindel (Bodley Head New Adults and Lions). It tells of zany, misfit Dewey and his love for Yvette, a freaked-out hippy who works with him. By slow degrees he realizes that Yvette's easy-going life in the commune can not give his life the meaning he is seeking. See also ZINDEL.

Arundel, Honor

An author of highly readable books about adolescent girls 'sorting themselves out'. Her particular skill is in portraying essentially selfish girls, without losing the reader's sympathies. Her most successful books show her heroines grappling with important decisions. In *The Terrible Temptation* and its sequel, *The Blanket Word*, a university student has to decide where her duty lies, whether to herself or to her family and friends who need her. In *The Longest Weekend*, an unmarried mother must choose between maintaining her independence, for the sake of her baby, or letting her own parents assume responsibility for the child. Other popular titles are *A Family Failing*, in which a girl asserts her independence as she accepts the realities of her parents' broken marriage; a trio of stories, *The High House*, *Emma's Island* and *Emma in Love* (all Piccolo) in which the girl of the title is shown maturing from a distraught adolescent to a self-possessed young woman. In *The Girl in the Opposite Bed* (Topliner) a snobbish spoiled girl gets her comeuppance during a painful stay in hospital.

It is this author's great gift of exploring problems without a hint of moralizing which makes her works so satisfying. (All titles are published in hardback by Hamish Hamilton.)

Asian Youth

The writer who chronicles most accurately the experiences of Asian teenagers in Britain is Farrukh Dhondy. His excellent collections of short stories, *East End at Your Feet* (Topliner) and *Come to Mecca* (Collins and Lions) which are about the day to day lives of Asian and

Black kids in London's East End are painful, funny and compassionate. See also his *The Siege of Babylon* under KIDNAPPING. Of appeal to readers up to thirteen is Jan Needle's *My Mate Shofiq* (Deutsch and Lions), a hard-hitting story set in the North of England about the friendship of a Pakistani boy with a white boy and the violence surrounding them caused by racial prejudice. Less satisfactory is *Tug of War* by Susan Gregory and Jill Tilling (Pyramid). Based on taped interviews with young people, it describes a few eventful days in the lives of two Asian teenagers. Unfortunately, the plot is a bit weak and the book suffers from a sense of having been written 'from the outside looking in'.

Baby Snatching

Three good books on this subject are of particular appeal to tender-hearted adolescents. For younger teenagers there's Noreen Shelley's *Faces in a Looking Glass* (OUP). This is as much about the effect which the kidnapping has on a small Australian community as it is about the girl's efforts to trace the baby. Particularly well-described are the girl's ambivalent feelings towards the baby's negligent mother. Older readers may prefer Joan Tate's *Sam and Me* (Topliner) which describes the events which drove a young wife to steal a baby. These are sufficiently convincing to persuade the doubting reader that the baby snatcher is not necessarily an inhumane monster, although this is the case in Catherine Storr's *The Chinese Egg* (Faber), because here the baby is kidnapped for a ransom. This is a subtle complex book which mixes fantasy with reality and which is also a penetrating study of relationships between a group of teenagers.

Black Experience

In recent years, there have been many books for teenagers concerning the Black experience – slavery, Black identity and Black heritage. The best of them take the reader further in understanding than the usual classroom titles on racial prejudice, such as *To Kill a Mockingbird*, Harper Lee, *Black Boy*, R. Wright and *Black Like Me*, J. H. Griffin. Julius Lester's *Long Journey Home* (Kestrel and Longman Knockouts) and *To Be a Slave* are selections of moving stories based on factual accounts of the hardships endured by Black slaves in

America. Equally harsh and moving is Paula Fox's *The Slave Dancer* (Macmillan and Piccolo), a harrowing account of life aboard a slave ship. More recent Black history is charted in *Roll of Thunder, Hear My Cry* by Mildred Taylor (Gollancz) a strong, compassionate story about the sufferings of a Black family in the South during the American depression. William Armstrong's *Sounder* (Gollancz and Puffin) shows the exploitation by the whites of a Black share-cropping family in the Deep South around the turn of the century. Some critics have condemned this book as 'racist' because, since all the characters are unnamed, it perpetuates the view that Blacks are lowly or inferior. Even more recent Black history is described in Julius Lester's *The Basketball Game* (Peacock, also contained in *Two Love Stories*, Kestrel). Here, the setting is Nashville, Tennessee, in the mid-1950s when racial prejudice and segregation were still rife. This is a poignant story of a young Black boy's friendship with a white girl and her ultimate betrayal of that friendship. Finally, here are three extraordinary, brilliant books by a Black American writer, Virginia Hamilton. Her poetic, sometimes dream-like works show present-day Black teenagers searching for their cultural roots and a sense of their own identity: *M. C. Higgins the Great* (Lions), *Arilla Sun Down* and *Justice and Her Brothers*, all published in hardback by Hamish Hamilton.

Blume, Judy

This American author's books are almost tailor-made for relieving adolescents' emotional hang-ups. Whether it's preoccupations with finding the right religion, as well as worrying about when you're going to start menstruating – *Are You There, God? It's Me, Margaret* (Gollancz); embarrassment about erections, wet dreams and a social climbing mum – *Then Again, Maybe I Won't* (Heinemann and Piccolo); what to do when your parents' marriage has fallen apart – *It's Not the End of the World* (Heinemann and Piccolo); how to have a responsible adult attitude to your sex life when you are only eighteen – *Forever* (Gollancz and Star). In all of these, Judy Blume offers the adolescent a refreshingly honest, humorous guide for survival. It's a pity there are so few like her writing on this side of the Atlantic.

Books For New Adults

A hardback imprint, launched in 1970 by The Bodley Head, of original fiction for teenagers aged roughly 14 to 18 years. This lively, varied list which comprises around 35 titles at the moment offers some of the best contemporary writing for young people by authors such as Gunnel Beckman and Paul Zindel. There are no concessions to the reluctant or less able reader here.

Brothers and Sisters

Here is a selection of titles which explore different aspects of the love/hate relationship between brothers and sisters. Sibling rivalry is often the main feature, although in the best of these books, the characters come to terms with their jealousy and acknowledge the underlying bonds of love and kinship. Already mentioned under BLACK EXPERIENCE are two challenging books by Virginia Hamilton, *Arilla Sun Down* and *Justice and Her Brothers* (both Hamish Hamilton). In the former, Arilla's jealousy of her radical elder brother lessens when, as the result of an accident, she begins to understand the inner forces which prompt his erratic, antisocial behaviour. In the latter, Justice is excluded from their lives by her twin elder brothers, until she realizes that they all share supersensory powers. Neither of these books is an easy read and it is very difficult, in a bare summary of the plot, to give any hint of the depth and richness of these works. In an altogether different mood is S. E. Hinton's *Rumble Fish* (Gollancz and Lions). Set in a tough American inner city, it's the story of Rusty-James, pool hustler and gang leader, and his attempts to model himself on his hero – his elder brother. The author points up the plight of kids who, as products of a savage, uncaring society, are destined to be losers, and at the same time, she makes some telling comments about the futility of violence. Lois Lowry's *A Summer to Die* (Kestrel) is a poignant story of a young girl coming to terms with the death of her elder sister, whom she resented yet admired. For older readers, Geraldine Kaye explores a similar theme in *Joey's Room* (Topliner). Mention must also be made here of Jill Paton Walsh's *Goldengrove* (Macmillan) the story of the relationship between two young cousins,. during the summer when they first begin to drift apart. This book seems to catch the precise moment at which a girl begins to leave her childhood behind. Its sequel, *Unleaving* (Macmillan), shows the same characters in adulthood, but this is a much more complex novel. It argues the case of emotions versus intellect, the vitality of love set against the rival claims of reason and logic. Heady stuff, when described in this way, but easier to comprehend in the context of the narrative. *Unleaving* is a brilliant book of ideas whose appeal is likely to be to a minority of teenage readers. Finally, Penelope Farmer's *Year King* (Chatto) a part fantasy about the stormy love/hate relationship of twin brothers which brings them near to tragedy. This is an oppressive, brooding book for very mature readers.

Bullying

There are some excellent novels on this theme. For starters, try Sam McBratney's *A Dip of the Antlers* (Abelard Schuman) about a lad with brains who refuses to knuckle under to the threats of the fifth form thug. Some of the moralizing is a bit heavy but the suspense is good. Barry Pointon's *Cave* (Bodley Head New Adults) is a much longer book on the same theme, weakling *v.* bully. It touches on other topics – the difficulty for a teenager of responding to the physical and emotional demands of the very young and the elderly. It's a good, straightforward story which has the added interest of motorbike mania. Nat Hentoff's *This School is Driving Me Crazy* (Angus and Robertson) is about an extortion racket in an American high school and the moral dilemma faced by the headmaster's son, also a pupil at the school, *viz.* 'to sneak or not to sneak' when he is implicated in the affair. Much of the book's success lies in the character of the boy's father, a man who is willing to sacrifice his son's welfare for the sake of his own high principles. From here, it's only a short step to one of the truly outstanding books of recent years, Robert Cormier's *The Chocolate War* (Gollancz and Lions). Again, it's bully-boy tactics in an American school, the rule of the mob and the huge bravery of one boy who dares to make his stand against the oppressive manipulators. This tough, uncompromising book, which is not for the squeamish, carries a warning which is relevant to the shaping of our attitudes to violence in society as a whole. Not to be missed. See also CORMIER.

Careers

The subject of how to choose a job or career is now dealt with much better in fiction than it was in the series of 'careers novels' which abounded in the 1950s and 1960s, and which are now, hopefully, dead. First, two enjoyable books by Prudence Andrew, *Goodbye to the Rat* and *Where Are You Going to, My Pretty Maid?* (both Heinemann Pyramids). These are sensible, down to earth stories about ordinary school leavers looking for jobs to suit their limited talents. Also in this series is Richard Parker's *Quarter Boy*, a light-hearted story about a lad who lands himself an unusual job – painting a figure on the top of the town hall. A head for heights is also needed by the hero in his first labouring job in *A Temporary Open Air Life* by Christopher Leach (Dent and Topliner). This book catches precisely the feelings of apprehension one experiences when starting work; there are some funny descriptions of leg-pulling rituals by workmates too. Joan Lingard's *The Resettling* (Hamish Hamilton) describes the difficulties encountered by a school girl when she helps to run her parent's plumbing business. *One of Barney's Girls* by Tom Browne (Topliner) dispels some of the glamour surrounding a trainee nurse's job, and the routines of office work are shown briefly but convincingly in Geraldine Kaye's *Marie Alone* and Delia Huddy's *My Kind of Cake* (both Topliner).

Perhaps the best book of all about an ordinary teenager at work is *Sticks and Stones* by Susan Price (Faber). It's the story of a lad's efforts to get the sack from his job at the supermarket so that he can become a gardener instead, contrary to his dad's wishes. This is a funny perceptive book about work and asserting one's independence. Finally, don't forget Barry Hines and *Kes* (Penguin) with its marvellous passage about the careers interview.

Cartoons

Hooray for cartoons and comic books – for Schulz's *Peanuts* in paperback (Coronet), for Goscinny and Uderzo's *Asterix* (Hodder) and for Herge's *Tintin* books. What a pity that Jean J. Loup's *Patatrac* (Cape) isn't available in a cheap edition. It's a glorious book-without-words which shows hundreds of funny people doing zany things, all on rich, colourful double-page spreads. Mind you, *Fungus the Bogeyman* by Raymond Briggs (Hamish Hamilton and Puffin) is available in paperback so that more than compensates. Few young people will be able to resist Briggs's Bogey world where young Bogeys read Anne of Green Bogeys and eat mouldy Flaked Corns for breakfast. Ugh! Marvellous inventive nastiness – it deserves to become a cult book.

Child Molesting

Not, you might think, a very likely topic for a book for adolescents, but there is an outstanding study of this subject in Nina Bawden's *Devil by the Sea* (Gollancz) which provokes sympathy for and understanding of the molester. A superb piece of writing for older teenagers.

Class

Here are a few books which look at class barriers. I dislike using the terms 'middle class' and 'working class', but they serve as useful shorthand here.

One of the best books on this theme is *The Breaking of Arnold* by Stanley Watts (Topliner Redstar) a bitter story about a working-class youth who 'betters himself' by self-education out of love for a middle-class girl, to no avail. The differences in background and class between the boy and the girl he runs away with are also crucial in John Rowe Townsend's *Good-night, Prof, Love* (Peacock), a perceptive story about adolescent love where, once again, the social barriers are ultimately too wide to be overcome. This is not, however, the case in Lynne Reid Banks's *My Darling Villain* (Bodley Head New Adults and Star) a straightforward romance about two young people from very different levels of socioeconomic background who fall in love. The strength of their feelings for each other over-rides the prejudices and misgivings of their parents, but neither young person has to betray his or her 'class' roots for the sake of the other – hardly credible, perhaps? David Rees goes over similar ground in *Quintin's Man* (Dobson). Finally, S. E. Hinton's *The Outsiders* (Gollancz and Lions) highlights the social differences between the haves and the have nots in a chillingly realistic story about rival gangs in the States.

Corlett, William

His trilogy *The Gate of Eden*, *The Land Beyond* and *Return to the Gate* (all Hamish Hamilton and the first and last also in Topliner) chronicles the emotional development of a man, from his adolescent friendship with an old man, and his first romance, through the aftermath of a broken love affair, to his own lonely old age in an authoritarian England of the near future. These are strange, dazzling books which are probably beyond the emotional grasp of many teenage readers – the second book is particularly difficult. See also KIDNAPPING.

Cormier, Robert

An American writer whose three novels listed here all make profound statements about society's malaise – in particular he questions our attitudes to violence and to human rights. See BULLYING; I AM THE CHEESE; KIDNAPPING.

Cults and Crazes

Books based on successful TV series and books which have been serialized on TV or made into a popular film are often the subject of short-term reading crazes amongst teenagers, so make sure you keep abreast of what's happening in these media. It would not be very useful to list here the latest 'in' books because they change so rapidly. However, a handful of books have reached the status of cult books which every literate, self-respecting teenager professes to know about, if not to have read: Richard Adams's *Watership Down* (Penguin and Puffin); J. R. R. Tolkien's Hobbit trilogy *The Lord of the Rings* (Allen and Unwin); and, increasingly, Russell Hoban's *The Mouse and His Child* (Puffin); Alan Garner's *Red Shift* (Lions) and Susan Cooper's *The Dark is Rising* (all five in Puffin). It's interesting that they are all fantasies.

Death

There are two outstanding books which describe the effect which the much-loved father's death has on a teenage girl: Jane Gardam's

The Summer after the Funeral (Hamish Hamilton and Peacock) and Mollie Hunter's *A Sound of Chariots* (Hamish Hamilton and Lions). In both cases, the girl's sense of loss is profound, and her grief is overcome only slowly and painfully. Coming to terms with the death of a sibling is dealt with convincingly in Lois Lowry's *A Summer to Die* and Geraldine Kaye's *Joey's Room* – see BROTHERS AND SISTERS. In *Risks* (Heinemann Pyramid) David Rees describes a teenage boy's anguish as he tries to piece together the reasons behind the murder of his best friend. John Harvey's *What About It, Sharon?* provides a disturbingly realistic picture of an average teenager who is so ill-equipped to withstand the pressures of her life that she contemplates suicide. *Is Anyone There?* edited by Monica Dickens and Rosemary Sutcliff (Peacock) which was published to commemorate the work of the Samaritans, is a collection of stories by well-known writers about these very pressures. In Gunnel Beckman's *Nineteen is Too Young to Die* (Topliner, published by Macmillan as *Admission to the Feast*) a girl who learns that she is soon to die from leukaemia looks back on her life and gradually comes to an acceptance of her situation. In the hands of a less able writer this could have been a piece of mawkish rubbish, but here Beckman's treatment is honest, unsentimental and deeply moving.

Delinquency

There must be dozens of books about teenagers who get into trouble with the law, but here I want to note just three books which explore in depth the root causes of delinquency. Unfortunately, none of them is available in paperback at the time of writing. First, Nigel Hinton's *Collision Course* (OUP) a remarkable novel about a boy who steals a motorbike on impulse, with tragic results. This is a realistic and compelling account of a boy wrestling with his conscience in order to justify his actions. Next, Roy Brown's *The Cage* (Abelard Schuman) a chilling account of unorthodox ways of reforming wrongdoers – it would be unfair to give away more of the plot than that. Finally, Christine Nostlinger's *Girl Missing* (Abelard Schuman) which examines the reasons behind a pretty, seemingly sophisticated teenager's decision to run away with her boyfriend from her mother and stepfather. The lessons to be learned here by weak parents are hammered home with too heavy a hand, unfortunately, but it's still quite a good read.

Dickinson, Peter

Peter Dickinson's talents as a writer for young people are many and varied. There is not the room here to list every title which could appeal to adolescents, but note *The Changes* (Gollancz, and published separately by Puffin as *The Weathermonger*, *Heartsease*, and *The Devil's Children*) these are science fiction/fantasy novels about a time when people have rejected the use of machinery; also *The Gift* (Gollancz and Puffin) a thriller about a boy who can see into the mind of a psychopath. See also HISTORICAL NOVELS and KIDNAPPING.

Didacticism

Didacticism is the scourge of much fiction for teenagers today. In the best fiction, the moral is implicit, but too many novels written for the adolescent market are written expressly to 'make a point' be it about social problems or what have you. Fortunately, most teenagers have acute powers to 'smell a rat' when a heavy moral looms, so they reject the offending book. Quite right too!

Dinosaurs

Dinosaurs are those books which, by rights, belong to a byegone age in writing, but which are still demanded by adolescents up to the age of thirteen. They are a sort of comfortable literary fodder, many of them published as long series and it's fashionable for compilers of lists like this to overlook them. Here are a few: Elinor M. Brent-Dyer's *Chalet School* stories (Armada); Helen Dore Boylston's *Sue Barton* stories (Knight); Carolyn Keene's *Nancy Drew* books (Armada); W. E. Johns's *Biggles* stories (Armada); Willard Price's *Adventure* series (Knight); F. W. Dixon's *Hardy Boys* books (Armada). And girls, in particular, still have leanings towards Blyton at this age occasionally.

Divorce

A pet theme for many writers of contemporary novels for teenagers is the emotional crisis young people undergo during the break-up of their parents' marriage, and when divorced or widowed parents remarry. Recommended for the reader up to the age of thirteen who has limited reading skills is Judy Blume's *It's Not the End of the World* (Heinemann and Piccolo), a straightforward account of how a young girl copes with her parents' divorce. For slightly older readers there is Geraldine Kaye's *Marie Alone* (Topliner) a gritty, realistic story about a girl whose father runs off with a younger woman. Vadim Frolov's *What's It All About?* (Macmillan and Topliner Redstar) is a more detailed account of the effects of marital breakdown. Set in Russia, it's an absorbing story of a boy's tangled emotions and disturbed behaviour when he discovers that his parents have separated without telling him. Anna-Greta Winberg's *When Someone Splits* and *When Someone Comes Along* (both Topliner) trace the effects which her mother's divorce and subsequent remarriage have on a fifteen-year-old girl. Although these two books occasionally sound as though the author intended them to show how model parents behave, i.e. unbelievably civilized, when they decide to divorce, they are still a good read. Finally, for younger readers, a wistful, poignant story about a young man who learns to forgive his feckless divorced father who rejected him, Paula Fox's *Blowfish Live in the Sea* (Macmillan and Puffin).

Earthsea

Ursula Le Guin's fantasy trilogy about Earthsea, *A Wizard of Earthsea, The Tombs of Atuan* and *The Farthest Shore* (all Gollancz and Puffin) has much to offer the adolescent reader who has tried and enjoyed fantasies by Garner, Cooper and Tolkien. Earthsea, the imaginary world she creates, is just as detailed and plausible as Tolkien's Middle Earth, and the weightiness of Ged the Magician's journeys, both physical and spiritual, are equal to those of Frodo Baggins.

Eccentrics

Eccentrics often seem to lead a much richer life than ordinary folk and they sometimes have something special to offer the teenager. Good fictional eccentrics who have a profound effect upon the emotional and psychological development of the young people with whom they interact are to be found in Paul Zindel's *The Pigman* and

Confessions of a Teenage Baboon (both Bodley Head New Adults and Lions) and William Corlett's *The Gate of Eden* (Hamish Hamilton and Topliner Redstar). See also CORLETT and ZINDEL.

Fantasy

The major fantasies for adolescents, or indeed for anyone, are mentioned elsewhere, but this list would be incomplete without some mention of the following authors whose works have much to offer young people.

Penelope Lively: probably her most complex use of fantasy is in *The House in Norham Gardens* (Heinemann and Piccolo), a rich, rewarding story about a girl's fantasies concerning an African shield.

Diana Wynne Jones: one of her best for the younger reader, up to thirteen, is *The Ogre Downstairs* (Macmillan and Puffin) a marvellous romp with a chemistry set which wreaks magical havoc on the youthful experimenters.

Patricia Wrightson: *The Ice Is Coming* (Hutchinson) a powerful fantasy on the grand scale, about a life and death battle between Australia's Old Forces of magic.

Fatties

For every fat teenager who longs to be thin the next book offers a ray of hope. M. E. Kerr's *Dinky Hocker Shoots Smack* (Gollancz and Puffin) a wickedly funny book in part about a fat, strong-minded girl who resorts to desperate measures to make her parents take notice of her. The author comments acidly on the lack of parental understanding which many young people suffer. Heroines who are fat, yet find boyfriends despite their fatness, are to be found in Sandra Rosenberg's *Will There Never Be a Prince?* (Topliner) and Maureen Stewart's *Orange Wendy* (Topliner), both a good, straightforward read.

Feminist Issues

There are three outstanding books which look specially at questions concerning the changing role and status of women in contemporary society: Gunnel Beckman's *Mia* (Bodley Head and Longman Knockouts) and *The Loneliness of Mia* (Bodley Head and published as *Mia Alone* Longman Knockouts). In the first book, Mia's suspected pregnancy leads her to formulate her own views about abortion and to question her chauvinist boyfriend's attitudes towards herself and her intended career. The second book looks at the whole issue of women's rights more closely, both in their own historical context, through the eyes of Mia's grandmother, and in the present through Mia's own views. Louise Fitzhugh's *Nobody's Family Is Going to Change* (Gollancz and Lions) is for a younger readership. It concerns an intelligent girl's efforts to persuade her parents to allow her and her brother to pursue the careers that they themselves want, rather than the career and roles which their parents regard as suitable. Despite the underlying seriousness of the theme, the book also explores children's rights and Black identity as well as sexist issues – the story is told with a lightness of touch which should make it accessible to a wide readership.

Friends

A newly-found freedom to choose one's own friends during adolescence can sometimes bring young people into conflict with their parents if they, the parents, think that the friends are 'unsuitable'. Here is a selection of books which look at some of the problems as well as the joys of friendship. Jean MacGibbon's *Hal* (Heinemann and Puffin) describes the friendship between a lively West Indian girl, leader of a gang, and the lonely younger boy whom she helps to recover from illness. A realistic novel which shows that true friendship involves responsibilities. Ivan Southall's *Bread and Honey* (Angus and Robertson) is about a thirteen-year-old boy's brief and often humiliating encounter with a little girl which teaches him much about himself, his values and his attitudes to conflict. This is a deeply moving book whose theories are expanded on in this author's *Josh* (Angus and Robertson and Puffin). Rosa Guy's *The Friends* (Gollancz and Puffin) is probably one of the most sensitive accounts of a friendship, despite parental disapproval, of two teenage girls. For other aspects of friendship see also NORTHERN IRELAND and OLD PEOPLE.

Gangs

For three widely differing views of teenage gangs, try Janet Green's *The Six* (Bodley Head New Adults and Longman Knockouts) six short stories, one told by each member of the gang, about key moments within and without the gang. These are by turns funny, tender and tough. Then sample S. E. Hinton's *The Outsiders* and *Rumble Fish* (Gollancz and Lions) for a much more violent picture of teenage gang warfare in the States. Note also the dynamics of the gang, including the struggles for leadership touched on by Barry Pointon in *Cave* (Bodley Head New Adults).

Garfield, Leon

Historical adventures, historical romances, call them what you will, there are now more than thirty of this distinguished writer's historical extravaganzas available to tempt the adolescent reader to the view that 'history' need not be dull. For those who need an easy intro-duction to his work, try one of his earlier books like *Smith* (Kestrel and Puffin) eighteenth-century London and the adventures of a youthful pickpocket; or the humorous *The Strange Affair of Adelaide Harris* (Kestrel and Puffin) skulduggery at a boy's academy, early nineteenth century. To bridge the gap between these and his full-length novels, there's *The Ghost Downstairs* (Kestrel and Puffin) a chillingly clever variation on the Faust theme, and the impressive series of 12 short books, *Garfield's Apprentices* (Heinemann and Piccolo). After that the reader should be ready for the fuller subtleties of *The Sound of Coaches* (Kestrel and Puffin) – the heyday of stage-coaches and the people who ran them; *The Prisoners of September* (Kestrel) – the French Revolution as seen by two young Englishmen caught up on opposing sides; and, best of all, *The Pleasure Garden* (Kestrel and Peacock) – love and intrigue in a larger than life re-construction of the Vauxhall Gardens. Perceptive readers will note that there is an underlying seriousness to much of Garfield's work, and that his best books make compassionate statements about man's corruptibility and the frailty of human emotions.

Garner, Alan

Two of his works of fantasy rooted in reality which get to the heart of adolescent emotions and relationships are *The Owl Service* and

Red Shift (both Collins and Lions). In the first book, three teenagers are involved in the present day re-enactment of a tragic Welsh legend. The second book, told in three parallel narratives, is in part a story of an adolescent relationship between a boy and girl in the present which has echoes and links with two groups of people in the past. Both these books demand that the reader works to extract the full meaning, but for those who persevere the emotional impact is tremendous.

Giftedness

The feelings of loneliness and the difficulties in communicating experienced by young people who are intellectually gifted are examined in *Bilgewater* by Jane Gardam (Hamish Hamilton) a wise, witty book about an ugly but clever girl's discovery that her sheltered upbringing has ill-equipped her to deal with her increasingly stormy emotions. Ursula Le Guin's *A Very Long Way From Anywhere Else* (Gollancz and Peacock) is the sensitive portrayal of a love affair between two gifted young people, both hitherto loners – suitable for mature readers. Prudence Andrew's *Robinson Daniel Crusoe* (Heinemann) for younger adolescents, is the story of the tragic effect wrought by his parents' continual pressure to 'do better' on a highly intelligent, ultra-sensitive boy. Finally, Alan Garner's *Red Shift* (Collins and Lions) a complex multi-layered book which shows, amongst other things, the destructive effect of the artist/thinker's lack of ability to communicate with, and relate emotionally to, the people around him. A challenging but deeply satisfying book for mature readers.

Historical Novels

A minority reading taste amongst teenagers, although publishers' lists would hardly seem to reinforce that view. The historical novels of Rosemary Sutcliff and Leon Garfield are dealt with separately in the main list, so here is a short checklist of other writers in this genre whose works are suitable for adolescents.

GILLIAN AVERY: mainly late-Victorian England, see particularly *A Likely Lad* (Collins) – self-help for a working-class lad.

HESTER BURTON: major events in English history, seventeenth to twentieth century, e.g. *Castors Away* (Puffin) Battle of Trafalgar; *In Spite of All Terror* (OUP) Dunkirk and the Battle of Britain.

PETER CARTER: Vikings, William Blake, Industrial Revolution, e.g. *The Black Lamp* (OUP) Peterloo Massacre.

GORDON COOPER: mainly domestic life, Edwardian to World War II, e.g. *An Hour in the Morning* (OUP) rural household prior to World War I.

MARJORIE DARKE: social history, eighteenth century to World War I e.g. *The First of Midnight* (Kestrel) slave trade, *Ride the Iron Horse*, railway age, and *A Question of Courage*, Suffragette Movement (Kestrel and Lions).

PETER DICKINSON: *The Dancing Bear* (Gollancz and Puffin) sixth-century Byzantium, *The Blue Hawk* (Gollancz) ancient Egypt perhaps, *The Tulku* (Gollancz) China, Boxer Rising.

ROSEMARY HARRIS: *The Moon in the Cloud, The Shadow on the Sun, The Bright and Morning Star*, trilogy about Biblical Egypt (all Faber and Puffin).

MOLLIE HUNTER: Scottish history, e.g. *The Stronghold* (Hamish Hamilton and Piccolo) Romans and Druids, Orkney.

ROBERT LEESON: family saga, Elizabethan times to Civil War in the trilogy *Maroon Boy, Bess*, and *The White Horse* (all Collins).

K. M. PEYTON: various periods, e.g. *Flambards, The Edge of the Cloud, Flambards in Summer*, Edwardian England and World War I (omnibus volume as *Flambards* OUP and singly Puffin). *The Right-Hand Man* (OUP) Regency England.

BARBARA L. PICARD: mediaeval society, knights, e.g. *Ransom for a Knight* and *One is One* (both OUP).

STEPHANIE PLOWMAN: Ancient Greece, Russian Revolution, e.g. *The Leaping Song*, Athens, and *Three Lives for the Czar* (both Bodley Head New Adults).

SUSAN PRICE: *Twopence a Tub* (Faber) 1850s pit strike.

MARY RAY: Classical World, e.g. *The Standing Lions* (Faber) Mycenaean period.

GERALDINE SYMONS: Edwardians, Suffrage, etc., e.g. *Mademoiselle* (Macmillan and Puffin) Warld War I.

GEOFFREY TREASE: Too many and varied to list. Most famous is *Bows Against the Barons* (Hodder) Robin Hood.

HENRY TREECE: various, but best are the Viking books *Viking's Dawn, The Road to Miklagard* and *Viking's Sunset* (all Puffin) and *The Dream Time* (Hodder) Bronze Age.

JILL PATON WALSH: Saxons in *Hengest's Tale*, Fall of Constantinople in *The Emperor's Winding Sheet* (both Macmillan and Puffin).

Horror

Horror stories and books about the supernatural hold a fatal fascination for many teenagers. There is an abundance of adult horror stories and ghost stories available in paperback, but for the young person who wants to try something equally chilling in the form of a full-length novel, there's John Gordon's *The House on the Brink* (Peacock) and *The Ghost on the Hill* (Kestrel) and Robert Westall's *The Watch House* (Macmillan) and *The Wind Eye* (Macmillan and Peacock). All these books are about sinister powers which menace and threaten to destroy the young people who awaken them. But they are far more than just ghost or horror stories because both authors are concerned primarily with exploring the inner tensions which motivate their characters.

I Am the Cheese

A stunningly original book by Robert Cormier which deserves to be read by everyone, not only by young people. The main narrative concerns a boy's journey to find his father, but it is punctuated by flashbacks and at first inexplicable interrogations so that the reader gradually realizes that the boy's situation is not that which was at first supposed. To reveal more of the plot would be unfair to the intending reader; let it suffice to say that the book is a sombre warning about our present society's frightening abilities to disregard the rights of the individual, and that it stands on a par with *One Flew Over the Cuckoo's Nest* (Picador) and Orwell's *1984* (Penguin). Cormier's book is published by Gollancz and as a paperback in Lions series.

It Can't Be Helped

It's difficult to think of any other book which covers the same ground quite so well – it's forthright and also enormously funny. *It Can't Be Helped* by Benjamin Lee (Bodley Head New Adults and Peacock) is the hilarious story of how a naïve young lad loses his innocence, both social and sexual. The hero's knack of putting a foot wrong at every single turn – in the headmaster's office, out on the sports field and even in his amorous cousin's bed makes for marvellously entertaining reading. Don't miss it.

Jews

Although there are many other books which chronicle the persecution of the Jews in Europe in the 1930s and 1940s, *The Diary of Anne Frank* (Pan) is probably still the book which speaks most directly to today's teenagers. However, for the reader who wants to pursue the theme further, there are two excellent stories about a Jewish family who fled to England from the Nazis: Judith Kerr's *When Hitler Stole Pink Rabbit*, suitable for readers up to about thirteen, and its sequel *The Other Way Round* for older readers (both Collins and Lions). Lynne Reid Banks provides a vivid picture of life in a kibbutz in *One More River* (Peacock) and her romantic novel *My Darling Villain* (Bodley Head New Adults and Star) touches briefly on the social pressures brought to bear by their Orthodox parents on two young people.

Kidnapping

Kidnappings and holding hostages – four superb books which give insights into the motives and emotions of both the abductors and their victims: Peter Dickinson's *Annerton Pit* (Gollancz and Puffin) is an adventure story with a touch of the supernatural about two young lads, one of them blind, who are held hostage with their grandfather in a disused mine. The motive for their being held is a political one, just as in *The Dark Side of the Moon* by William Corlett (Hamish Hamilton). This is a much more difficult book suitable for mature readers. The story of a teenage boy's abduction from his boarding school is told in parallel with that of an astronaut's solo flight to the moon – not as weird as it sounds, because each of the characters is shown facing his own private terrors during the periods of isolation. Farrukh Dhondy's *The Siege of Babylon* (Macmillan and Topliner Redstar) is a gripping story of a siege lasting several days in which three young West Indians hold captive a group of hostages. Through a series of flashbacks, the reader learns the past life of each of the captors – lives which have been as directionless as the ghettos which bred them. This is an angry, eloquent book which says much about the reasons behind the rebellion of young Blacks today. Finally, Robert Cormier's *After the First Death* (Gollancz) which is a stunning novel about terrorism in which an urban guerrilla holds a busload of small children hostage. There isn't the space to tell more about it than that – just read it, then you'll understand why it's probably the last word on this subject.

Love

Here's a half-dozen of the best books about adolescent love which have been published specially for teenagers recently. They describe the joy and pain of falling in love for the first time, but they also suggest, realistically and honestly, that first love is unlikely to last for very long. Ursula Le Guin's *A Very Long Way From Anywhere Else* (Gollancz and Peacock) is already noted under GIFTEDNESS. It is a short, moving book which explores the question of whether or not one has to feel truly committed to someone before agreeing to have sex. Judy Blume's *Forever* (Gollancz and Star) is already noted under BLUME. It is a straightforward love story which is particularly good for the frank, unsentimental way in which it deals with sex. Barbara Wersba's *Tunes for a Small Harmonica* (Bodley Head New Adults) is a funny poignant story about a sixteen-year-old who falls hopelessly for her poetry teacher, with spectacular consequences. Paul Zindel's *My Darling, My Hamburger* (Bodley Head New Adults and Lions) is a bittersweet story about the relationship of two high school couples which should reinforce the young person's view that one's parents' attitudes towards love and sex are not necessarily the best for oneself. Deborah Hautzig's *Hey, Dollface* (Hamish Hamilton) is a frank, unpatronizing story about two teenage girls who are sexually attracted to one another, although it's never actually stated that they are lesbians. This book celebrates the fact that, to become aware that one is ultimately responsible for one's own definition of sexuality, marks a major step towards full maturity. *The Tent* by David Rees (Dobson) makes the same statement, only this time the protagonists are male.

Mental Illness

Several of Roy Brown's novels contain characters who are mentally handicapped or disturbed. The best of these which centres on a police hunt for a missing psychotic girl is *Find Debbie* (Peacock, published also as *The Siblings* by Abelard Schuman). This book highlights the problems of living with the mentally ill and at the same time uncovers the deceptions practised by the parents of the handicapped child. Note also Brown's sensitive portrayal of a backward, disturbed child in *The River* (Abelard Schuman). Bernard Ashley deals sympathetically with the special needs of the autistic young person in *The Trouble With Donovan Croft* (OUP and Puffin). Note also Jill Paton Walsh's sensitive contribution to our understanding of attitudes towards the mentally handicapped in *Unleaving* (Macmillan) and Max Lundgren's treatment of a mongol child in *Summer Girl* (Topliner). Probably one of the most convincing studies of how it actually feels to be mentally ill is *The Summer Before* (Macmillan and Topliner Redstar). This is the story of a young girl's nervous breakdown brought about by the death of her boyfriend. The author conveys successfully the feelings of deep depression, confusion and isolation which the girl experiences as she slowly regains her health.

Newlyweds

There are few really good books about teenage marriage on publishers' juvenile or young adult lists, presumably because works which explore this subject are thought of as adult books. However, the following books give the young person real insights into the adjustments which 'young marrieds' must make if their relationship is to survive. Joan Lingard's *Into Exile, A Proper Place,* and *Hostages to Fortune* (all Hamish Hamilton, the first two also Puffin). These books, which should be read in this order, follow on from earlier stories, *The Twelfth Day of July* and *Across the Barricades* – see under NORTHERN IRELAND. They chart the progress of the marriage of Protestant Sadie and Catholic Kevin as they learn to cope with the tensions brought about not only by numerous moves of home and the birth of their baby, but also, more fundamentally, by their differences in religion and political upbringing. K. M. Peyton's *Pennington's Heir* (OUP) gives a less than romantic view of wedded bliss, as the hard-up young couple struggle to make ends meet while the husband begins his uncertain career. Ardent feminists would probably criticize all the young women in the stories listed here for the passive roles which they assume.

Northern Ireland

Here are three thought-provoking books which look at the violence and prejudice unleashed by the Protestant and Catholic troubles in Ulster. All of them show that the mindless prejudice which divides the hearts of men is a tragedy. Joan Lingard's *The Twelfth Day of July* and *Across the Barricades* (both Hamish Hamilton and Puffin) trace the friendship, and later love, which develops despite the barriers of differing religions and political upbringing between a Protestant girl and a Catholic boy. Peter Carter's *Under Goliath* (OUP) also covers the clandestine friendship of two young people from opposing 'sides' – this time two boys. This is a much more satisfying book than the first two because the characters are more believable.

Old People

These four books all show the special bond which may develop between a teenager and a grandparent or other elderly person. Susan Price's *Home From Home* (Faber) is a funny, touching story about a lad who adopts an old lady as a granny substitute, because his own mum hasn't much time for him. Paul Zindel's *The Pigman* (Bodley Head New Adults and Lions) describes the progress of a teenage boy's and girl's friendship, made by chance, with a lonely old man. It's a tender, funny, compassionate book with a tragic ending – see also under ZINDEL. Joan Lingard's *The Clearance* is the first of four books which chart the emotional development of a spirited teenager, Maggie McKinley (all published by Hamish Hamilton). In this one, the special friendship which Maggie shares with her Scottish grandmother is sympathetically explored. Finally, William Corlett's *The Gate of Eden* (Hamish Hamilton and Topliner Redstar) also noted under CORLETT is a retrospective account of the friendship between an old man and an adolescent boy told through narrative and letters. A sensitive book for mature readers.

Parents

The difficulties of fully understanding one's parents and asserting one's independence of them are treated particularly well in M. E.

Kerr's *The Son of Someone Famous* (Gollancz and Peacock). The young man of the title, a high school dropout who can't live up to his father's expectations, changes his name and goes to live with his grandfather. The friendships which he makes help him to understand his father a little better. A quietly humorous book. Paul Zindel's *Pardon Me, You're Stepping on My Eyeball* and *Confessions of a Teenage Baboon* (both Bodley Head New Adults and Lions) show mixed-up American teenagers trying to overcome the psychological damage done to them by their awful parents – see also ZINDEL. William Mayne's *A Game of Dark* (Hamish Hamilton) is a terrifying story, part fantasy, part reality, about a boy's emotional conflict with his crippled father. This is also one of the themes in Aidan Chambers's *Breaktime* (Bodley Head New Adults) although here the treatment is much more realistic. See also XPERIMENT.

Peacock

Peacock Books was the first paperback series designed specifically for teenagers in this country. It was launched by Penguin in 1962 and at present there are about fifty novels and a dozen non-fiction titles on the list. Most of the novels have already been published in hardback editions. Only books of the highest literary merit are included in the series, which contains 'adult' as well as 'teenage' novels, so Peacocks represent top quality writing, usually of appeal to a fairly literate adolescent audience. Key authors in the list include John Rowe Townsend, M. E. Kerr, and Jane Gardam.

Physical Handicap

Two books which describe intelligently and sympathetically the bitterness and frustration felt by young people who are physically handicapped are Myra Schneider's *If Only I Could Walk* (Heinemann Pyramids) in which a disabled girl, confined to a wheelchair, leads a fuller life in college than she had anticipated, and Cordelia Jones's *The View From the Window* (Deutsch) which presents the long stay in hospital of a girl who is crippled by rheumatoid arthritis and is helped by new friends to view her disabilities in a more positive light.

Pyramid

Pyramid Books, a series launched in 1967, now comprises more than fifty short novels in hardback for teenagers. Most of the titles were commissioned for the list which aims to attract young people who do not readily enjoy books, i.e. the reluctant reader. The emphasis is on stories about today's teenagers, although there is nothing controversial in them – no explicit sex in any of the romances. The standard of writing is usually competent, so the list provides safe, but satisfying reading material for those with limited reading skills.

Quests

Several writers have used the theme of a journey undertaken by young people to 'see the world', or at least a part of it, as a device to show the teenager learning about his or her identity and formulating attitudes and values about life in general. The best of these are Adrienne Richard's *Into the Road* (Gollancz) in which encounters with Hell's Angels, 'blessing of the bikes' ceremonies and lots of other experiences on the road with his elder brother convince a boy that there is a world of difference between being a 'biker' and just a boy with a bike. John Craig's *Zach* (Gollancz) is an absorbing account of a young American Indian's journey across America and Canada to find other members of his lost tribe. Dorris Heffron's *A Nice Fire and Some Moonpennies* (Peacock) describes another Indian teenager's encounters with sex, drugs and lots more besides, during a short visit to the city. A very funny book this one. So too is John Crompton's *Up the Road and Back* (Topliner) a story about a young man who, bored with the factory routine and his inability to get very far with his girl friend, hitches lifts to Scotland in the hope of learning a bit about sex on the way. He does too, but not in the way that he expected.

Religion

Not a very promising theme at first sight for teenage novels but there are two very good accounts of young people's wonderings about their religious beliefs, namely Judy Blume's *Are You There, God? It's Me, Margaret* (Gollancz) and Peter Dickinson's *The Tulku* (Gollancz).

School

Most of the books about school life are listed under BULLYING, but there are two other outstanding books which need to be mentioned in this context. Kenneth Wood's *A Period of Violence* (Dobson), a brilliant story about the damaging effect of a too-strict headteacher on the life of the pupils and teachers in his school. Seen through the eyes of one of the pupils, the message of the book is that violence begets more violence. Alison Prince's *The Doubting Kind* (Methuen and Topliner Redstar, two volumes) already mentioned under ADDICTION, provides a vivid picture of school seen through the somewhat jaundiced, cynical eyes of two bright schoolgirls.

SF

Andre Norton is the doyenne of SF writing for young people. Only two of her many novels are available in Puffin: *Beast Master* and *Catseye*, but these should whet the appetite. Try also John Christopher's Tripods trilogy: *The White Mountains*, *The City of Gold and Lead* and *The Pool of Fire* (all Hamish Hamilton and Beaver) about a time in the future when earth is dominated by mind-manipulators from another planet. Louise Lawrence's *The Power of Stars* (Collins and Lions) is also about alien powers controlling people's minds, but the setting here is contemporary. Robin Chambers's *The Ice Warrior* (Kestrel and Puffin) is a collection of very original SF short stories. For older, more mature readers, try Louise Lawrence's *Andra* (Topline Redstar) a frightening picture of life 2000 years hence, and even more moving is Jan Mark's *The Ennead* (Kestrel) which describes life in a totalitarian state on a distant planet which, as all the best SF should, carries a statement about our own society underneath.

Sutcliff, Rosemary

She is the writer of historical novels *par excellence* and probably needs no introduction here, although for many young people that may not be the case. If teenagers have not already experienced her books, try a relatively easy one first, such as *Tristan and Iseult* (Bodley Head and Puffin) a haunting retelling of the great tragic romance.

A minority of readers will then want to move on to her superb books about Roman Britain beginning with *The Eagle of the Ninth* (OUP and Puffin) and to *Sun Horse, Moon Horse* (Bodley Head) early Iron Age, and then *Blood Feud* (OUP and Puffin) Europe in the Dark Ages.

Topliners

A non-net paperback series launched in 1968 by Macmillan Education for teenagers. It now comprises well over a hundred titles, mainly fiction, with an emphasis on originals and some translations, particularly from Scandinavia. Arguably, this list has become one of the most popular in British schools day, not only because of its scope and size – it covers everything from SF to 'problem novels' – but also because most of the stories are told in a fairly direct style, 'accessible' is what the blurb says. For teenagers with mature reading skills, the books in the Topliner Redstar series offer challenging reading. Taken as a whole, this is a very good series which provides a wealth of material to encourage the adolescent reader to read more.

University Life

A student's life at university today may not be quite so carefree or abandoned as that portrayed by Kingsley Amis in *Lucky Jim*. For a more realistic, down to earth picture of happy studentship try these three thoughtful novels which show young people coping with their new life at university – making new friends, fitting in with academic routines, and adjusting to the demands of living away from home and family for the first time. Honor Arundel's *The Terrible Temptation* and *The Blanket Word* (both Hamish Hamilton) life at Edinburgh University as seen through the eyes of a determined, somewhat self-centred young woman; and Rodie Sudbery's *Ducks and Drakes* (Deutsch) the last of a series of five titles about Polly Devenish which trace her life from early childhood as shown in *The House in the Wood* to the last one which shows her as a student at York University.

A Very Long Way

. . . *From Anywhere Else*, although this superb love story by Ursula Le Guin has already been mentioned, it really does deserve some extra attention, just in case you should miss it (Gollancz and Peacock).

Westerns

For the fans of horse operas and spaghetti westerns here are two books which give a more realistic picture of the Wild West. John L. Foster's *Westward in Their Wagons* (Topliner), short stories about crossing the prairies in wagon trains. Charles Portis's *True Grit* (Peacock) a classic story about a girl who determines to find her father's killer. John Wayne fans will probably remember the film. For a more up to date view of cowpunching try Adrienne Richards's *Pistol* (Gollancz and Lions) which gives a convincing picture of the life on a ranch in Montana during the Depression.

Xperiment

Several writers noted in this list are experimenting with form as well as content in their works. For example, Alan Garner in *Red Shift*; Robert Cormier in *I Am the Cheese* and *After the First Death*; and Aidan Chambers in *Breaktime* all make use of fractured, non-sequential narrative. Both Aidan Chambers and Robert Cormier invite the reader to participate in games, so that the reader is warned from the outset that the book's plot is probably not what it seems. Aidan Chambers and Paul Zindel have presented parts of their texts in unusual ways by using facsimiles of letters, cartoons, visual puns and typographical innovations.

Xanadu Manuscript

The Xanadu Manuscript by John Rowe Townsend is an SF story, not the type of book one normally associates with this author. Basically, it's a time travel story about a family from the future who come to stay in present-day Cambridge, but the author is as much concerned with the effects which their visit has on the people they meet in the present as on their own adjustments to our twentieth-century world. It's all very neatly done and often illuminating. On the subject of the future, here is as good a place as any to note this author's bleak look at a not too distant future in *Noah's Castle* (OUP and Peacock). Set in a time when England is bankrupt and people are starving, it examines the moral dilemma of a boy whose father has hoarded food for his family, but for their use only. A sombre, thought-provoking book.

Xenophobia

A book which has proved to be successful with adolescents, although it was intended for a slightly younger readership, is Jan Needle's *Albeson and the Germans* (Deutsch). The plot concerns a young lad who is afraid of what the German kids will do to him – he's read in comics that they might even eat him, and he believes every word. He is persuaded to vandalize the school. He does it very well.

Young Mother

Looking back from our vantage point in 1979, when our teenage literature covers virtually every topic from homosexuality to urban terrorism, in varying degrees of verisimilitude, it is perhaps difficult for us to appreciate the controversy which the publication in 1965 of this, to our eyes, fairly innocuous book by Josephine Kamm aroused. But at that time, the publication on a juvenile list of a book about a pregnant, unmarried girl represented a real breakthrough in that it considerably extended the range of topics which could be examined in books for adolescents. It's still in print (Hodder) but it no longer seems to be in tune with society's attitude towards unmarried mothers, and that's putting it mildly.

Zindel, Paul

The last entry here, but really his books should come first, because they are probably the best of all novels for and about teenagers. They nearly all concern young people who are alienated from their parents, who are disenchanted in some way with the world around them and who, at the outset, are unable to communicate their emotions. Don't all young people feel these things at some stage? His books are seldom happy, but then, how can they be, when they so often concern young people who are low in self-esteem and high in anxieties – these brought about usually by parents who are either utterly selfish or who are suffering serious personality disorders themselves. But that is not to say that the books are without hope. The hope lies in the hands of the young protagonists to shape and mould their own destinies. Zindel speaks directly to teenagers both in the subjects he chooses to write about, and in the actual way he writes. His style is very intimate and the numerous jokes, visual puns, typographical innovations and asides to the reader grab and hold the attention. Here, then, is a list of his books in published order all of which should be on the bookshelf of every teenager in the land. They are published in hardback by Bodley Head New Adults and in paperback by Lions, all except the last one. *The Pigman, My Darling, My Hamburger, I Never Loved Your Mind, Pardon Me, You're Stepping on My Eyeball, Confessions of a Teenage Baboon* and *The Undertaker's Gone Bananas*.